MY JOURNEY

UNDER

HIS WINGS

Pursuit for Freedom

I was helped to publish my book by...

www.authorshub.ca

DEDICATION

Primarily, I give praise and honour to The Most High Ahayah Ashar Ahayah, acknowledging Him as the only Power I worship and revere. Through His Son Yashaya and The Holy Spirit, He is the One who strengthened my faith and taught me to rely on Him and His ability to protect and secure me under His Wings throughout this journey.

This testimonial account of my journey under The Most High's Wings is dedicated, first, to my father, Rev. Pumelele Mandlamakhulu Mpumlwana, and my mother, Nomonde Ethel Mpumlwana. Both my parents passed on to be with our forefathers and hopefully resting in Abraham's bosom. However, it is important to note that it was through their prayer support during this journey that I can now write about this testimony. My father instilled in me, very early in my life, to always read and pray Psalm 91, the scripture which has been used as the main reference for this book.

Secondly, I dedicate this book to my beloved brother, Loyiso, Khanyisa Bunye Mpumlwana, who is also resting with our forefathers. He and his wife Nyameka Ruth Mpumlwana also had to flee to exile from South Africa after suffering torture and imprisonment by the Apartheid regime.

Thirdly, my dedication goes to my three daughters, Nambitha Nomthandazo, Pumela Truth, and Nompumelelo Nomonde, who, by default, became part of this journey. I am also grateful that The Most High saw me through it all and later gave me a son, Nkululeko Samuel.

ACKNOWLEDGEMENT

I would like to acknowledge and thank The Most High God for His divine guidance and protection as I journeyed in the pursuit of freedom, His Son Yashaya, and The Holy Spirit for urging me to document this journey under His Wings. I also want to acknowledge and thank those Christian Leaders who in the last decade have been bringing forth sound uncompromised teachings of the Gospel of Christ. Listening to these teachings inspired me to find my identity.

ORIGIN AND MEANING OF UNCOMMON WORDS USED IN THIS BOOK

The following names and phrases are used in this book interchangeably:

Ahayah Ashar Ahayah or Ahayah: This is the Hebrew translation of the Name of God – I AM THAT I AM, which was given to Moses in Exodus 3:13-14 (KJV).

AHAYAH: a short version of Ahayah Ashar Ahayah.

THE MOST HIGH GOD OR POWER: This expression will sometimes be used in reference to Ahayah or God Almighty.

YASHAYA: Hebrew word meaning MY SAVIOUR (e.g., in 2 Samuel 22:3). This is the name of Christ or The Messiah, the Son of the God of Israel, who is popularly referred to by many as Jesus.

A-BANTU ABANGONI; NGUNI; BANTU: Shemitic Hebrew race in South Africa, often referred to as Bantu or Nguni people; a shortened version of A-Bantu Abangoni – Literally meaning, the people who do not sin. People of The Law. This is based on the understanding that sin is the transgression of the Laws, Statutes, and Commandments of The Most High. These people will sometimes be referred to as Negroes or Blacks

AFRIKAANER: The Caucasian race of Dutch, German, or Huguenot descent who live in South Africa. They speak a Dutch dialect called Afrikaans and are also known as Boers.

COLOUREDS: A mixed race of people, the majority of who live in the Western Cape Province of South Africa.

INDIANS: These are the people of East Indian descent whose majority live among the AmaZulu Bantu tribe in South Africa.

Table of Contents

JOURNEY UNDER HIS WINGS 1

INTRODUCTION..2

CHAPTER 2 COURT TO KNOCK..................................22

CHAPTER 3 THE JOURNEY OF THE THREE BEGINS...28

CHAPTER 4 THE LAST MEAL IN OUR HOME COUNTRY 34

CHAPTER 5 FINDING THE WAY TO "FREEDOM"...42

CHAPTER 6 TESTING THE MOMENTS OF "FREEDOM" 52

CHAPTER 7 LIFE IN THE "FREE WORLD" BEGINS ..58

CHAPTER 8 CHANGING HANDS 66

CHAPTER 9 THE WOODS LIFE EXPERIENCE 74

CHAPTER 10 THE FISHING TRIP OF NO RETURN ..78

CHAPTER 11 FROM CASA DE MORTE TO PRISON .92

CHAPTER 12 PRISON, A GLORIFIED CASA DE MORTE..96

CHAPTER 13 PERSUIT OF FREEDOM THROUGH EDUCATION..104

CHAPTER 14 MY ORIGIN, MY TRUE IDENTITY.....116

CHAPTER 15 DESPERATE PRAYER IN SEARCH OF THE TRUTH 122

CHAPTER 16 KNOWING ONE'S IDENTITY: A KEY
TO FREEDOM 130

APPENDIX...136

JOURNEY UNDER HIS WINGS

Psalm 91

He that dwelleth in the secret place of The Most High shall abide under the shadow of the Almighty.

I will say of the Lord, He is my refuge and my fortress: my God; in him will I trust.

Surely he shall deliver thee from the snare of the fowler, and from the noisome pestilence.

He shall cover thee with his feathers, and under his wings shalt thou trust: his truth shall be thy shield and buckler.

Thou shalt not be afraid for the terror by night; nor for the arrow that flieth by day; nor for the arrow that flieth by day;

Nor for the pestilence that walketh in darkness; nor for the destruction that wasteth at noonday.

A thousand shall fall at thy side, and ten thousand at thy right hand; but it shall not come nigh thee.

Only with thine eyes shalt thou behold and see the reward of the wicked.

Because thou hast made the Lord, which is my refuge, even The Most High, thy habitation;

There shall no evil befall thee, neither shall any plague come nigh thy dwelling.

For he shall give his angels charge over thee, to keep thee in all thy ways.

They shall bear thee up in their hands, lest though dash thy foot against a stone.

Thou shalt tread upon the lion and adder: the young lion and the dragon shalt thou trample under foot.

Because he hath set his love upon me, therefore will I deliver him: I will set him on high, because he hath known my name.

He shall call upon me, and I will answer him: I will be with him in trouble; I will deliver him, and honour him.

With long life will I satisfy him, and shew him my salvation.

INTRODUCTION

Life is a journey that begins with The Most High God's decision to release a soul to the earth, encasing it in human form, male or female. He knows each one of us even before we are conceived in our mother's womb. King David testified of this fact in Psalm 139:

> *Your eyes saw my uninformed substance, and in Your Book all the days [of my life] were written, even before they took shape, when as yet there was none of them. (verse 16, KJV Bible).*

When the father and the mother of all mankind, Adam and Eve, were first created, The Most High God gave them FREEDOM and made them King and Queen to rule over all creation. After they fell to sin, freedom could not be taken for granted. All of mankind strived, and still continue to strive to regain freedom at all costs, through righteous or unrighteous means.

Righteously, by observing and obeying the laws, statutes, and commandments of The Most High God, as in the example set by Enoch, Methuselah, Noah, Shem, Abraham, Sarah, Rebecca, Judith, and other righteous men and women who lived on this earth including Yashaya Christ, the anointed Son of The Most High.

Although unrighteous methods could not lead to freedom, mankind, it seems, has always maintained a facade, thinking that forcibly keeping others under their subjection would, in turn, give them a sense of freedom. In parallel, those who are made subjects through oppression would continue to rebel and, at times, violently engage intermittently in futile struggles against their oppressors, with hopes of gaining **"FREEDOM."**

The challenge begins when we pursue our journey in this world without understanding The Most High God's purpose for our lives. This major challenge is also tied to the fallen nature of the very bodies into which we are born; along with the deception of the age which we grow to accept as the truth; thus, keeping us in ignorance about The Truth.

We journey through this life without sight unless, of course, we submit to the Will of The Most High by laying down our lives and, most certainly, our will. This is precisely what Our Savior Christ did when He entered this world through His earthly body, well-articulated by the Holy Spirit through David in his Psalm:

Then I said, Behold, I come; in the volume of the book it is written of me; I delight to do Your will, O my God; yes, Your law is within my heart. (Psalm 40:7-8)

In this book, I write about my own personal journey to "freedom," which began when I fled from the then-oppressive

Apartheid Caucasian government of South Africa in 1975. What is certain is that in the process of this journey, The Most High, in His sovereignty, steered my life in the direction that ultimately led me to the point of surrendering to the Lordship of His Son, Christ. I believe through the reverent prayers of my parents, along with His grace, mercy, and faithfulness, The Most High God, purposed to allow me to journey under His Wings, where I could always find refuge.

I relay the part of the journey when I was at the beginning of my prime life and going through much trepidation and harsh molding of self. I trust this testimony will encourage many who are walking aimlessly, without the truth like I was, and perhaps to a large extent, I still do not fully understand the real meaning of freedom.

This part of my journey began during the time when the South African youth, under the Apartheid government, was again visibly resisting the oppressive laws of the country that disadvantaged mostly non-Caucasian citizens. Although the oppressive laws could be felt at various levels by those who were referred to as "Non-Whites," most brutality was targeted towards those who were referred to as Bantus or A-Bantu.

South African youth of generations before our time had a track record of revolting against the unjust laws that were imposed by the oppressive Caucasian South African governments. These include people like Mandela, Sobukwe, and Mbeki (the senior), to mention but a few.

In 1975 there was a new kind of tension in the country, which was fueled by the victory won by our brothers and sisters in

Mozambique. They fought against the Portuguese colonial government under the leadership of Frelimo and their leader Samora Moises Machel. This victory brought hope among the young people in South Africa, which fueled a new determination to fight and overthrow the heavy yoke put on by the Apartheid regime.

Nevertheless, little did I know that The Most High God was to use my active involvement in this resistance movement to take me out of South Africa on a journey Under His Wings. Yes! I was to undertake a journey of no return, through which The Most High, His Son Yashaya, and the Holy Spirit would eventually reveal the real reason why I and my people, A-Bantu, in South Africa were serving under the heavy iron yoke of the Caucasian rulership. In addition, and most importantly, was to learn how to free ourselves from this iron yoke.

In this book, I will walk you through the path of my journey of no return. I will also attempt to explore the concept of freedom, perhaps from my perspective; from the South African A-Bantu's viewpoint; as well as from The Most High's perspective.

Lastly, I hope to demonstrate how I later understood why my journey under His Wings was important, how it turned and transitioned to my benefit and His purpose, and how it was divinely arranged and hence could not be avoided.

Relevant Characters At The Beginning Of My Journey

The two main people with whom I left the country were Joel and Monica. Joel had returned from Botswana (a neighboring country) a few days earlier, where he had met with one of the African National Congress (ANC) leaders. ANC was, at the time, one of the liberation movements that opposed the South African Apartheid government. He was instructed to recruit and lead people who would be interested in joining the liberation movement outside South Africa.

Monica had recently been released from detention (prison) two weeks before I met her at our Alexander township (i.e., Ghetto) underground house. The "underground" referred to a hiding place for people who were actively participating in the planning or in the carrying out of strategies used to oppose the then Apartheid South African government.

The third important person was Zach, Monica's boyfriend. Zach was the father of Monica's baby, whom she miscarried in detention during her brutal torture. Zach was also an ANC underground member whose assignment was to help transport ANC recruits to cross any of the South African borders to neighboring countries. Monica and I were, however, unaware of Zach's ANC-related assignment. He kept it confidential for security reasons. I am not sure, though, if Joel was also not aware of Zach's assignment since they were both ANC members.

The fourth person was Tom. We had met him for the first time at one of our underground meetings a night before a court day we were to attend. This event will be mentioned in the next chapter. Tom was not well known to us.

Lastly, Justin was a trusted comrade who was still living within communities and who often updated us on the latest information regarding our police-detained comrades.

CHAPTER 1

GROWING UP UNDER LEGALIZED RACIAL SEPARATION

I was born in the Eastern Cape Province, the part of the country where people speak a Xhosa dialect. Xhosa was one of the kings whose brothers were Ngqika and Gcaleka. As it was a practice among A-Bantu, sons often took on the names of their fathers generationally. Therefore, Xhosa, being the king over these communities, his name, over time, was used to identify the developed dialect spoken by people in his kingdom.

Although I was born in a village, at the age of eight years, my family moved to the city of East London, where we lived in a township (ghetto). This was an area that was designated for A-Bantu and was separated from other racial groups. Life in our community was a struggle. It was normal to see parents leaving their homes incredibly early morning and rushing to Caucasian families in the suburbs to work as domestic servants or to go to do factory work. I remember observing children in some homes in my neighborhood using verandas (balconies) as bedrooms due to limited space in their two-roomed homes. People in my community simply made the best out of difficult living circumstances. The education we received was designed for blacks and called Bantu Education.

After completing my high school education, I enrolled in a nursing school, which was an extension of one of the hospitals catered for A-Bantu. Although nurses in training consisted of A-Bantu, Indians, and Coloreds, most of the teachers were Caucasians. Nevertheless, races were never mixed; the A-Bantu were separated from the other two groups. Our instructors were Caucasian women, and of course, this was to be my first experience ever having a Caucasian person as a teacher.

During our first three months, our teachers would instruct us to fill up bathtubs with water and take turns scrubbing each other thoroughly. We were informed that, by nature, our skin was dirty because of our brown pigmentation. We had to be obedient to this rigorous demeaning process as it was our passage to the actual nursing training.

Student nurses were accommodated in a dormitory-style hostel. The main floor of this hostel accommodated only Indians and Colored student nurses, while A-Bantu were on a different floor. Although teachers were not accommodated in the same building, they were always present at mealtimes. Naturally, our menus were differentiated according to our races. Caucasians always had a high grade of meat, vegetables, and whatever starch was served for them. Indians and Coloreds had the second-best choice of food.

I recall the days when we had meat on our menu; it would be difficult to tell whether we were getting pork or beef or a combination of different kinds of animal flesh. At times we would be served with stakes made from soybeans.

It goes without saying that salaries for student nurses were also based on racial classification; A-Bantu received the lowest on the scale. In fact, my monthly salary for the first year of training in 1971 was R50, an equivalence of about $5. As one can imagine, this amount could hardly take care of my personal needs as a young woman. I remember calling my father every month and asking for financial help to make ends meet. As time went on, I could sense the strain and burden I was putting on my father, who also was doing everything he could to take care of his ministry needs as well as taking care of his household.

The Miracle Money

One day, I decided to attend an Anglican chapel service that was offered to student nurses on campus. On that day, I gave an offering of a 25-cent coin, and it felt 'good.' It was the end of the month, and I had just been paid my salary. The following Sunday, I again planned to attend the service, but this time I had no money to offer. I then remembered the testimony my father once shared with me when he was young. He would go out to a field not far from his home, dig on the ground, and find a British five pennies coin. [South Africa at the time was using British pound currency.] He shared that he would take this money to the church as an offering. If he went back to the spot on any other day, he would not find money except for when he was to attend church service. He shared that after a few weeks of experiencing this miracle, he decided to use the money to buy candies (sweets). Well, the following week, when he went to dig in the same spot, there was no money to be found.

I decided to try my father's money miracle-making secret. I felt in my spirit to go to our laundry room and went straight to the drainage hole of the sink. I found a 25-cent coin and used it as my offering. In my mind, I needed a miracle of a large amount that could also supplement my meager salary. For the next three Sundays, I found the same amount in the same spot and offered it. When I began to use the money for my personal need, the miracle ceased.

I recall talking to one of my friends who was a year senior than me in nursing training. She was slightly lighter in skin color than me but was visibly not of mixed race. She informed me that she and her immediate family had to change their last name by translating their Xhosa family name into Afrikaans (the language spoken by Caucasians of Dutch descent). She informed me that since she and her family lived in Cape Town, where most people of mixed race lived, she was able to enjoy some of the privileges A-Bantu could not access. These privileges included relatively better education, higher salaries, better housing, etc. Indeed, she was paid a much higher salary than any of A-Bantu student nurses. Since she qualified as a third-class colored, I am not sure though whether she received the same salary scale level as the first or second-class coloreds. Third-class coloreds were light in complexion like many A-Bantu can be; they had kinky hair and similar features as all of us. Coloreds were classified from first-class category to third-class category depending on how closely their physical features resembled a Caucasian.

This segregation was practiced within the hospital environment as well. As Bantu student nurses, we were trained to always stand on the sideway whenever a Caucasian registered nurse was approaching and passing by. We had to take off our warm covering capes during the winter season, put our arms behind our backs and bow as the Caucasian nurse passed by. This might sound ridiculous and far-fetched to our youth readers who were born on or after 1994, the year of the so-called freedom in South Africa.

Nevertheless, one thing I could not fully understand was the reason why people of my race had to be treated less than mankind in the eyes of our oppressors, particularly by the Caucasian race in South Africa.

Evidently, one of the former Prime Ministers of Apartheid South African government articulated their justification for this continuous oppression and slavery over the Bantu people in his statement as follows:

The following is part of the speech made by former South African President P.W. Botha to his Cabinet. This reprint was written by David G. Mailu for the Sunday Times, a South African newspaper, dated August 18, 1985.

"............... We do not pretend like other Whites that we like Blacks. The fact that Blacks look like human beings and act like human beings does not necessarily make them sensible human beings. Hedgehogs are not porcupines, and lizards are not crocodiles simply because they look alike. If God wanted us to be equal to the Blacks, he would have created us all of a uniform colour and intellect. But he created us differently: Whites,

Blacks, Yellow, Rulers, and the ruled. Intellectually, we are superior to the Blacks; that has been proven beyond any reasonable doubt over the years. I believe that the Afrikaner is an honest, God-fearing person who has demonstrated practically the right way of being."

See Appendix for the rest of the speech.

Well! then, is there hope for

A-Bantu or the Shemetic Negro race to ever obtain freedom?

Yes, I was born and grew up in a society where this racial hierarchy was legalized, normalized, and appeared to be accepted. In fact, conditions like poverty, hard, cheap labor or glorified slavery, low standards of living, sicknesses and inflicted "incurable" diseases, young age, high death rates, etc., were and still are mostly associated with A-Bantu in South Africa. This is the reality today, despite the so-called freedom and democracy which was supposedly attained in 1994.

I always wondered what the real justification is for the so-called Blacks or Negroes as a distinct nation to be subjected to harsh laws of oppression and slavery by other nations of the world. What could be the reason for these people to always be associated with incurable diseases and poverty in large proportions in comparison to other races of the world? What can be the reason for all this unending suffering?

The pressing question is, did Negroes in South Africa get the freedom they needed in 1994? If our living circumstances have not significantly changed, except for the few elites, can there be Freedom for A-Bantu or Negro race? Did I and all freedom fighters who were in and outside South Africa accomplish what we set out to obtain, to free our nation from our endless suffering? If the answer is NO, as evidence proves to be the case, maybe we need to get a better understanding of what freedom means for the negroes and how to attain it.

Resistance Against The Yoke Of Bondage

Look! A-Bantu in South Africa had, over many years, done everything they knew to resist this oppressive maltreatment in "their own country" but without success. This resistance is understood to have started in the 17th century, about 1652, after the arrival of Caucasians from the Netherlands, Portugal, Germany, and the British Islands. The indigenous people who were also in the region at the time, the Khoikhoi African people, were the first to resist the aggressive invasion of these Caucasian settlers. Subsequently, the rest of the Southern African region became a blood-flooded ground as A-Bantu resisted through bloody wars until they were subdued. Slavery of our people who were shipped through the Indian and Atlantic oceans to Europe, Asia, Arab countries, Brazil, and the Americas became part of our history. The reader is encouraged to visit the slave museum in Cape Town, right under the parliament building.

Nevertheless, the invasion of Southern Africa (Angola, Zambia, Namibia, Mozambique, Zimbabwe, Botswana, and South Africa, including Lesotho and Swaziland) by European Caucasians and other nations increased. Our people continued to suffer harsh oppression under the Caucasian taskmasters and ultimately through legal segregation systems.

Despite these harsh laws which were put in place to hold down A-Bantu under servitude, we never gave up fighting for freedom but continued to resist in different forms. These included non-violence political organizations, which later became militant "liberation" organizations, public protests, and through awareness songs, etc.

In the process, some leaders were incarcerated and put in long-term imprisonment (such as Mandela, Sobukhwe, etc.). Others were brutally tortured and killed while in police detention (such as Biko, Mohapi, etc.). Some were assassinated (such as Tiro, Hani, etc.). Many were hung with ropes while in prison; others were gun-shot and killed during public protests.

Consider the 1960 Sharpeville Dom-Pass (an identity book-like document which was designed to be used only for Negroes in South Africa) protest, which resulted in a massacre for our people by the Afrikaner Apartheid government; the 1976 Youth nation-wide protests during which many young people were brutally killed while others were exiled; 1982 Maseru massacre by South African Apartheid soldiers. All these sufferings are for the hope of attaining "freedom" for A-Bantu.

In observing the Negro communities or A-Bantu in other African countries, including the Americas, who were also visibly colonized, enslaved, and oppressed by Caucasians and/or Arab nations, I then began to see similarities in how as a people, we were treated, irrespective of where you were born and lived in the world.

In most, if not in all of these African countries, great leaders like Nkruma in Ghana, Lumumba in Congo, Nyerere in Tanzania,

Nojumo in Namibia, Mugabe in Zimbabwe, Kenyata in Kenya, Machel in Mozambique, to mention but a few, had to put up resistance on behalf of their communities, against Caucasian and/or Arab colonial masters.

Despite their resistance which for some cost them their lives in the process, all Shemetic Negro communities are still remotely or directly controlled, economically and politically, by these colonial nations.

Poverty, high rates of unemployment, diseases, and high death rates of young people have become the norm and are often associated, by and large, with A-Bantu or so-called Africans. Consider the undeclared or unrecognized worldwide holocausts and genocides of our people.

These include genocides in Rwanda; Namaqualand (today's Namibia); genocide of the so-called North American Indians, who originally had negro features. Undeniable observation is that negro-looking people, as well as the so-called Hispanics, seem too often to get the short end of the stick wherever they live. In fact, there is a common understanding among A-Bantu that "if you are Black, you will always be treated without respect, dignity or honor, irrespective of where you are in the world."

All the while, Christianity, in various forms, had been and can still be regarded as the main religion upheld by most of our people in South Africa. One can find churches in almost every street of ghettos, villages, townships, and squatter camps (informal settlements) where A-Bantu reside. Surely, over centuries, many have believed and still believe that these religious institutions like Christianity and Islam might "hopefully" bring solutions or at least bring relief to our suffering. In fact, some of A-Bantu would mix Christian beliefs with ancestry worship. Others focus solely on ancestry worship, spirit medium often referred to as Sangoma, divination, and animal sacrifice to the dead, all with the hope of finding solutions to the endless suffering.

I recall in 2016 asking one of the Caucasian church leaders in South Africa why our people continue to suffer even after the so-called 1994 "political independence." To my surprise, she told me that the reason for our suffering has to do with our genealogy as Hamites, the cursed race. This leader said we are the descendants of Ham, whose grandson Canaan was cursed by his grandfather after Ham had dishonored his father Noah (Genesis 9: 22-26). Thus, the curse trickled down to us because we are of the Hamitic lineage.

This leader informed me further that there is nothing much we could do about this curse except we repent and cleanse our family bloodline all the way up to Nimrod, "our forefather." Thus, failing to do so, the curse on us and our descendants was permanent without any hope for deliverance. This explanation sounded logical and **deep** to me since I never took time to study the biblical history of the nations of the world.

Mind you, I had been a Christian all my life and had been taught that Christ, who became the ultimate and perfect sacrificial Lamb, had atoned for my sins. I had understood that by believing in Him and having faith that He had redeemed me, I would be freed from any curse. I never asked this leader why Christ's sacrifice could not atone for my inherited curse from Canaan and Nimrod.

Nevertheless, I did not hesitate to join in when some of the church leaders of this ministry were helping people to cleanse their bloodlines. I also went through my bloodline cleansing, repenting with the purpose of removing the curse I supposedly inherited through being the descendent of the wicked Nimrod, who rebelled against The Most High God. I desperately needed solutions for myself and for my people, who continued to suffer endlessly despite all other efforts they used to obtain freedom in South Africa. To this end, I volunteered to stand in the gap and did a bloodline repentance on behalf of my Xhosa-speaking group in South Africa.

Well! Despite the repentance, my circumstances and those of our people remained unchanged. I began to realize that something was not adding up for me in relying on or totally believing in this understanding. I also wondered if the Apartheid regime and some of the Caucasians in South Africa had this understanding that A-Bantu were the cursed Hamites who deserved to be dehumanized, which probably justifies their oppressive actions.

I am convinced, though, that my Caucasian Christian leaders meant well and never purposed any malice against my people and me when they told me that I was a Hamite. It seems this was and perhaps is a popular understanding among Caucasians in South Africa and globally that A-Bantu or people of Negro race are of Hamitic lineage. It also made sense that almost all nations of the world, particularly the Western World, benefitted from our legalized oppression in South Africa. Nevertheless, one thing I could not fully understand was the reason why my people had to be treated less than mankind in the eyes of our oppressors, particularly by the Caucasian race in South Africa.

Yes, I was born and grew up in a society where this racial hierarchy was legalized, normalized, and appeared to be accepted. In fact, conditions like poverty, hard, cheap labor or glorified slavery, low standards of living, sicknesses and inflicted "incurable" diseases, young age, high death rates, etc., were and still are mostly associated with A-Bantu in South Africa. This is the reality today, despite the so-called freedom and democracy which was supposedly attained in 1994.

FREEDOM OR TRODDEN HORSE?

I believe gaining freedom was a quest for most of our people, whether they could covertly or overtly make this desire known. As I have noted earlier, in the course of time, many of our people who attempted to fight for the freedom inside South Africa were incarcerated, tortured, and brutally killed. Many others had to flee to other countries as refugees, while others left the country for the purpose of getting military training. This latter group had intended to return to South Africa to physically fight to attain freedom for the oppressed Bantu people.

On the other hand, the then so-called 'known enemy,' the Boers (Afrikaners or Caucasians), used everything in their power to keep our people at the lowest level of servitude. They used psychological warfare, drug warfare, as well as brutal means to keep us a base.

At last, the enemy of our people resorted to effective psychological warfare by bringing into our communities a trodden horse. This was in the form of giving us the so-called "independence" on a platter, which in the natural mind meant victory and "freedom at last." This they did by releasing Nelson Mandela from "prison," a man who was upheld in high regard as the true leader by our people, a form of Moses or the Messiah if you will.

Trodden horse? How? One might ask. Well, when I went back to visit South Africa in 1994, the year of declared "Freedom," I observed that our people had begun to entertain high hopes. They, so to say, were building castles in the air about how at last, their living conditions were going to drastically change for the best.

Today, almost 30 years later, most of the Bantus are in a dire state of poverty and unemployment. They are dying at young ages of diseases and violence. Most of the Bantu traditional lifestyle is almost eradicated, leaving young people living a lawless untraditional lifestyle with no proper direction.

All the while, Christianity, in various forms, had been and can still be regarded as the main religion upheld by most of our people in South Africa. One can find churches in almost every street of ghettos, villages, townships, and squatter camps where A-Bantu reside.

Surely, over centuries, many have believed and still believe that these religious institutions like Christianity and Islam might "hopefully" bring solutions or at least bring relief to our suffering. In fact, some of A-Bantu would mix Christian beliefs with ancestry worship. Others focus solely on ancestry worship, spirit medium often understood as Sangoma, divination, and animal sacrifice to the dead, all with the hope of finding solutions to the endless suffering.

In the following chapters, I will walk through my journey under His Wings. I will also attempt to provide biblically based facts for what, in my opinion, true freedom is for A-Bantu and how to possibly attain it.

CHAPTER 2
COURT TO KNOCK

"All stand," a stern voice sharply commanded as an Afrikaner Judge walked into the courtroom wearing his robe and a tailed wig on his head. The trial of some of our brothers, who had been detained in prison for several months, was to begin in one of the Pretoria courtrooms that morning.

My four friends and I had emerged from our "Alexander Township underground" to attend the trial in support of these brothers. Joel had just finished sharing the details of his new assignment with excitement and had expressed hope that we were going to be his first recruits when Justin walked into our hiding place. His countenance looked sad as he began to inform us that our friends were to be in court the following morning. We knew the court hearing was only a formality to pass sentence and officially grant the police legal right to have our brothers locked in prison for a long time, during which they would experience more brutal torture or death. We all knew the reason for Justin's sadness, as some of our brothers and sisters in our group had already experienced prison torture.

While the comrades were figuring out how we could attend the court proceedings, my mind was preoccupied with Joel's assignment and troubled by his intention to have us all leave the country. Although I was not quite sure what joining a liberation movement outside South Africa meant, I knew that it would not be easy for me to come back home.

I had had enough of living a life on the run. I knew I did not feel ready to leave my small children and family behind to venture out into the unknown. "I still have some time, though, to think it through," I thought, "and perhaps to visit my family in the Eastern Cape Province." I also had hopes that I could find another hiding place that was closer to home. I could then make frequent visits to my family without being noticed by the police.

Notwithstanding, we finally decided to tough it out and went to attend the court proceedings. We dressed up for the day to look presentable. I proudly put on my traditional Xhosa dress, making a statement of how proud I felt to be a Bantu. Monica and I also took a change of casual clothes, which we intended to change into at the end of the court proceedings. The idea of going back to the township wearing formal clothes felt uncomfortable since we did not want to stand out within our community.

Court drama

It was not long after the judge had settled down when Monica pulled me to the side and nervously told me to quickly jump through a low but big opened window that was at the back of the courtroom. We were the last two of the five in our crew who were at the courthouse to exit through the window. Zach had stepped out and positioned a pick-up van (small truck) right under this window for the rest of us to jump onto it. As soon as Monica and I jumped onto the van, Zach drove off speedily, winding the one-way streets in downtown Pretoria.

Noticing that we had uninvited company (i.e., the police) following us, Zach quickly swerved the vehicle onto a side street and drove fast, disregarding speed limits. The notoriously known 'special branch' police also increased the speed following behind us. It was so silent in the van that you could hear the heavy breathing of some of the comrades. The tension and fear of what we all imagined would happen if the police were to catch up with us were written all over our faces. Yes, they could shoot and kill us or take us to detention and mercilessly torture us.

Monica held my hand tightly. I began to imagine the thoughts going through her mind, "another detention?" She had just been released from detention only two months earlier and had already experienced brutal torture from this special police. She had not fully recovered from the trauma she had suffered through detention and torture, during which she also miscarried.

OH! We lost them as we disappeared into Mamelodi Township and proceeded towards the East towards the Mozambican borders. We all just took a sigh of relief and began to talk about what had led to this unplanned dramatic journey of no return.

In my mind, I kept wondering what might have led to this sudden drama. Right then, Joel began to inform us that he had spotted two police in private clothes pointing at us and overheard them planning how they were going to arrest us. We all knew what that would entail. It didn't take much those days for people to be taken into detention indefinitely and be brutally tortured, sometimes to death, just because of suspicions. This was common practice, particularly towards those who were classified by the Apartheid regime as Bantu(s) ... Kaffirs, and/or non-white.

The excitement of our successful escape and anticipation of a free and better life ahead of us was evident in the zeal with which we loudly sang freedom songs. All this was abruptly interrupted by a sudden loud noise from the front of the van. What could that be? We all exclaimed, rather shocked.

Zach stopped the vehicle to check the source of the noise. Agh! yerhe-e! he exclaimed, choking from the smoke that greeted him as he opened the front hood. We all jumped out to see what the problem could be. The worst had happened, the oil tank had dried up, and the engine head "knocked," that is, it was damaged. The worst indeed!

What the rest of us didn't know was that Zach had taken the vehicle from a friend who worked for the South African Counsel of Churches (SACC), with the understanding that it would be returned to the office by early afternoon that same day. We were now about two hundred miles away from the city of Pretoria. There was no obvious way of getting back on time, let alone returning it in a drivable condition.

LO AND BEHOLD, THE LOT FALLS ON

Mozambique had just obtained its political liberation from the Portuguese colonial presence. Therefore, it would have been a reasonably preferred and safe neighboring country to go to for South Africans who, at the time, needed refugee status. I could not admit I was ready at the time, as I still had my secret plans to visit my family and possibly hold back for a little longer in hiding. Well! Zach's assignment to take us close to the Mozambique borders ended suddenly, with the engine failure.

The fifth person in our company was Tom. Monica and I had bad vibes about him. We just didn't trust him. There was something in me that gave me a feeling that he could be a secret agent for the government. In the first place, it did not make sense to me that the special branch police would give up so easily on chasing us without a backup plan. In my mind, Tom was their backup plan, period! Could it be that the breaking down of the car was Ahayah's divinely executed plan to protect us?.... Just a thought.

Nevertheless, we had to come up with a quick solution, the sun was going down, we were in the middle of nowhere, and the car needed to be towed back to the city. One of us had to hike back to Pretoria to get help. Guess who the perfect person could be to get this job, Tom.

It was important for Zach to remain with the car until it was returned to the SACC. Joel was the main contact with the outside world, so we depended on him. As females, Monica and I could not be asked to venture back to the city. **LO AND BEHOLD! THE LOT FALLS ON TOMMY.**

CHAPTER 3
THE JOURNEY OF THE THREE BEGINS

He shall cover thee with His feathers, And under His wings thou shall trust; His truth shall be thy shield and buckler. (Psalm 91:4 KVJ).

A Good Samaritan Positioned

Joel, Monica, and I were left with no other choice but to start hiking toward the nearest place we could go to hide, leaving Zach waiting for whatever available help he could find. We arrived at Manyeleti Game Reserve at about nine o'clock that evening. By now, our stomachs were growling, not having had anything to eat since the previous night. We had a few Rands (South African currency) to secure a room for that night.

Ahayah had positioned one of His "Good Samaritans," Mthembu, to welcome us. A very hospitable man indeed. He gave us a meal free of charge and two rooms for one room's price. We quickly made friends with this man. He seemed to empathize with our plight even though we had not disclosed our plans to him. I figured he had seen a few like us passing through several times. He put his job on the log as he managed to support us with room and board for the following four days until we became conspicuous to the management team of the resort.

Signal To Move On

On the eve of the fourth day, one of the white staff members asked Monica, in the Afrikaans language, who we were and what we were really doing at the reserve. Afrikaans is the language spoken by most Caucasians and Coloured communities in South Africa.

Since Monica was a Coloured, it was no surprise that the man would speak to her in the language. Clearly, this became a signal for us to move on; we could smell trouble coming.

MOVE ON! WHERE TO? HOW DO WE BEGIN?

I seemed to be the only one with this question, perhaps a reflection of my concealed fear of the unknown. Mh-h, where is my faith? I quietly reprimanded myself, "After all, I am the only one who confesses to being a Christian here among us, even though I haven't attended any church service for months," as if that mattered much to The Most High. Had I fully committed my life to Ahayah and His Son Yashaya Christ at the time, I would have at least been encouraged by this Bible verse that has become my favorite scripture today:

"For ye have not received the spirit of bondage again to fear;
but ye have received the Spirit of adoption, whereby we cry,
Abba, Father. (Romans 8: 15; KJV)

In realizing that his white colleague was being suspicious, Mthembu quickly advised us to leave. Certainly, his kindness was likely going to cost him his job and another opportunity to assist others like us who would probably be coming through.

Ubuntu (Kindness): Ahayah's Favor Revealed

It was on a Sunday morning when we finally left the Manyelethi Game Reserves. Mthembu had made sure we had a good breakfast, enough to sustain us to the next meal ... not sure when that would be. However, I figured that if The Most High Ahayah could feed the prophet Elijah by employing ravens to bring daily portions of meals, and later through a widow woman, as recorded in 1Kings 17:4-9 and 1Kings 17:4, surely, He would sort us out without any doubt. This was the kind of private conversation that was going on between my mind and my spirit. Somehow it strengthened my faith and kept me going.

We walked all day, not being sure of the direction we were heading. At about sunset, a man driving a vehicle stopped and offered us a ride. He told us that it was too dangerous to walk in the area and that we could easily get killed by the police or soldiers.

During our conversation with him, this man, who later introduced himself as Theko, realized that we were trying to find directions to leave the country. He then took us to his home as the day was already spent.

This is the kind of hospitality you would get from people who live further away from the cities. This act of kindness is referred to as Ubuntu, a phenomenon with which I was familiar, having grown up on a family farm near a small town. Theko knew right then that we were planning to 'skip' the country (this is the term used when people were leaving the country with intentions to join the liberation movements outside South Africa). He brought us into his small two-roomed house, which was on Roman Catholic Mission grounds, and asked his wife to prepare us a meal.

He then asked a Black catholic priest who lived next door to his house to accommodate Monica and me while he had Joel stay with him. Theko told the priest that Joel was his cousin who had come from the city to visit him, I was Joel's girlfriend, and Monica was my close friend. This seemed to work for a while.

A Mission Within A Mission

Theko knew the area well, including a relatively safe path that we could use to cross the border fence that was between South Africa and Mozambique without having to go through the border gate. He offered to explore the safest path for us, a task that seemed to be quite difficult to undertake. This was because the path Theko knew was close to the Kruger National Park, one of the most popular holiday resorts.

Evidently, the path stretched along the fence that was heavily patrolled by the South African soldiers. Nevertheless, Theko would be up early in the morning daily to go "scout" the area, but coming back with not a promising report.

Although it was becoming a frustrating task for him and a cause for panic, clearly, it was not safe for us to venture out. By the end of that week, the priest who was hosting us had many questions to ask; he was becoming suspicious that we were on a mission that could put their Catholic Mission in trouble with the government. Theko had to pretend to be unaware of our mission when the Black priest shared his suspicion with him that we appeared to be involved with the liberation movement.

As the priest was getting ready to BLOW THE WHISTLE on us, we left before dawn on a Saturday, heading out towards Swaziland. Theko had done all that he could to help. However, it was becoming obvious that keeping us for longer than he had would put him and his family in danger.

The night before we left the Catholic Mission, Theko had pointed out the direction we needed to take to get to Swaziland, a neighboring country to both South Africa and Mozambique.

It would be a long way, he cautioned, but that it would be much safer than crossing the fence to Mozambique near the Kruger National Park. We quietly left the premises of the Catholic Mission before dawn at dusk; it was so dark we could hardly see a bush five hundred meters away. We were almost bumping into each other as we walked, and we had no clue of the direction we were taking.

I began to have my usual silent prayers, asking The Most High to lead us. I recited my favorite childhood Psalm 23, mumbling under my breath:

".....THY ROD [TO PROTECT] AND THY STAFF [TO GUIDE], THEY COMFORT ME".

I felt sudden calmness and peace, an experience I could not share with my comrades. As the beauty of the dawning light began to appear, we got excited to see a small village at a far distance. It felt like we had been walking for about six or seven hours by the time we got to the first home. Mind you, none of us had a watch to check the time, nor did we have a compass for directions.

CHAPTER 4
The Last Meal in Our Home Country

Tea hit the spot

As we were approaching the village we had seen miles away, we were greeted by herds of cattle, flocks of sheep and goats, being driven by shepherd boys. It was a small village that was settled by few family homes. We went to the first home we could get to without wasting time, feeling very thirsty and famished. On arrival at this home, we felt warmly welcomed by a kind woman who introduced herself as MaMaseko. We also introduced ourselves, giving her false names to conceal our identity in the event that the police attempted to track us down. We then told her that we were on our way to Swaziland to a relative's funeral and that our car had broken down; hence we had to walk the rest of the way.

Walking long distances was not foreign to villagers, so our story was believable. We asked her for some water. While we were drinking, she quickly put a kettle of water on a primus stove (a burner fueled with paraffin).

She proceeded to prepare breakfast and served us hot tea that had fresh milk from the cow and fresh bread that had been made that morning. I've had tea many times in my life, but there was something different about this one. It just **'hit the spot'** in such a unique way that it left me with long-lasting memories.

Could this be our last meal in this land?

Was this our last meal in the land which we had known as the home of the "Bantu nation," as the land of our ancestors? This question crossed my mind. A feeling of grief paralyzed me for a moment. I remembered the last meal I had with my father in Queenstown, Eastern Cape Province, where he served as a minister of the Gospel. I had gone to visit him shortly before I went to Johannesburg. He had no idea that I had been harassed by the police. He knew that my work had to do with a Home Industry in a village called Njwaxa near Alice, a small town close to King William's Town.

At the time, I was a member of the Black Consciousness Movement (BCM) under the leadership of Steve Biko, a once-famous South African political leader who later died in prison detention under the brutal hands of the Apartheid regime. I had been assigned to create jobs for the villagers by training them to make leather products, such as belts, bags, and sandals. Most of these people had some of their family members incarcerated in Roben Island (prison) for an extended period as political prisoners.

While I was at this BCM project, I had several visitations by a special branch of the police who were known to harass and detain people they suspected to be a threat to the government. During their first visit, they had warned me to "watch my back" because they believed that the project was only a camouflage for underground political activities. I had avoided other visitations by running to hide as soon as we saw their vehicle approaching from a distance.

The Lord's Supper For the Last Meal

Hiding within the village was becoming too dangerous. I was running out of secure places to hide. I decided to leave the area altogether for fear of getting detained by the police. It was at this point that I went to visit my father as I needed his blessings.

Although I spent a night at my parents' mission house, I could not tell them that I was planning to travel to the big city of Johannesburg, nor did I tell them about my experience with the police. The next day, my father convened the usual early morning family prayer meeting, which this time included Holy Communion or the Lord's Supper. His prayers and blessings were somehow different. He spoke prophetically as if he knew that this was going to be my last meal with him. Indeed, it was.

A Loaf Of bread and a Bottle Of Water

It was about ten in the morning by the time we arrived at MaMaseko's house. The sun was already pouring its heat at its gradual pace. We needed to take advantage of the daylight and begin our adventurous trip. As soon as we finished having our breakfast, we asked MaMaseko if she or any of the people in the village could help us with directions. She called one of her relatives, a man who had worked for one of the Afrikaner farmers in the area, to give us directions. He mentioned two ways from which to choose, a short path that would require us to go over the Drakensburg mountains or a longer way that could take us three days to get to Swaziland. We had to make a quick decision on the suitable route to take. Well, the kind lady equipped us with a loaf of fresh bread and a bottle of water.

This provision reminded me of when Abraham was instructed by Ahayah in Genesis 21:14 to send Hagar, his bondwoman, and his son Ishmael away. Yes, she gave us provision, our last meal as we were to leave our homeland behind.

Although the food was not our primary focus at this point, I couldn't help entertaining ungrateful thoughts, "OK, REALLY! what is a loaf of bread and a bottle of water going to do for three grown-ups on a very long journey?" Nevertheless, it was a very kind gesture, and we were truly grateful for her generosity. In this, I perceived Ahayah's love and His purpose that was beyond our understanding.

Yes, one loaf of bread and a bottle of water are enough when seen through spiritual eyes. After all, our **KING** Yashaya Christ did feed five thousand men with only five loaves of bread and two fish. Heck! one could also say, "half-a-loaf is better than no bread" when it gets down to it.

Mountain Climbing

We had to make a choice quickly; we needed to get out of South Africa as soon as possible before we could get caught by the police. Taking a long way to avoid the high Drakensberg mountains was, for a moment, appealing, at least to Monica and me, but obviously not to our advantage. The choice became clear; MOUNTAIN CLIMBING! THE WAY TO GO.

We began heading towards the mountain direction, a trip of about an hour's walk from the village. We took courage and began the climbing, not an easy task, particularly for Monica, who could have easily weighed about 190 pounds. The sun seemed to enjoy targeting our unprotected heads. At least we still had some little water left in the bottle to wet our throats.

Somehow, we gained strength and made it to the top. We sat down and finished whatever was left of the bread, threw the empty bottle away, and rested for a while. By this time, I had also thrown away my heavy traditional Xhosa outfit.

We began to slowly descend to the other side of the mountain slope. By the time we reached the bottom, the sun had begun to go down. We had done it! No one was complaining of tiredness; it felt like we had been carried by the Angels. At the bottom of the mountain, we saw a wide gravel road that looked like it was well-traveled, probably by Afrikaner farmers who lived in the area. Although we were somewhat hesitant to take the road, fearing that we could become easy targets, we also had no other choice but to take it and hoped that it would lead us to Swaziland. At this point, one thing was certain in my mind; we had no control over this journey, and clearly, The Most High, Ahayah, was leading us.

Reassuring Vision within a dream

As dusk was setting in, we proceeded to walk on the winding gravel road, with a forest on our left side, stretching about five miles. It had grass long enough for us to imagine the presence of wild, dangerous snakes and animals. I recall a few times when each time a vehicle appeared behind us, we would throw ourselves right into the grass and roll into the trees to hide, not thinking about the danger we might fall into.

We finally passed the forestry area, but we continued to walk until our feet became very tired. It was probably past midnight when we finally decided to take a rest. Ahayah had provided a bright, full moon that helped us to see the way.

We sat down on a short grass by the road and fell asleep. The Lord gave me a vision within my dream. A Bantu-looking angel in the form of a man who seemed familiar came to me, holding a huge dog on a leash. He said these words, "My child, you are now leaving home. Do not be afraid I will be with you".

I woke up and jumped onto my feet. Noticing that dawn was about to break, I woke my friends up, so we could continue with our journey. Although I was a bit shaken and overwhelmed by my dream, my friends didn't notice, and I didn't care to share my experience with them either. I felt energetic, encouraged, and with a strong determination to fearlessly move forward on the journey.

Awe! Owch! Yo-o! Please help!

We began the day feeling refreshed and eager to push until we crossed over to Swaziland. Although we had no idea how challenging it would be, we were certain that it would be less dangerous than trying to cross to Mozambique. We took advantage of the early morning breeze and walked as fast as we could. Joel was leading ahead of us with his long male strides. I was following close behind him when suddenly, I heard, "Awe! Owch! Yo-o! wait for me, please." I looked back and saw my friend Monica rolling her back on the ground and holding her right foot high up in the air. I helped Monica to her feet, but she could not stand. She had sprained her ankle. 'Now what? We have no time to waste; we need to make this our final day in South Africa.' As these thoughts ran through my mind, I hollered at Joel. He stopped, looked back, and sat down.

I had hoped he would offer to carry Monica or at least support her, but he didn't seem interested. Although I knew I hardly weighed 120 pounds, I felt determined to carry her on my back and continued at a slower pace for a while.

The Most High had us under His wings.

The task of carrying Monica was becoming so challenging that we decided to rest and plan how we were going to proceed. We were not sure if it was a sprain, a minor fracture, or simple exhaustion. We were hoping for the latter, which would be easy to solve. **REST** became the best option. As we were still thinking of the next possible step to take, Monica spotted a cave right next to where we were sitting. What a perfect place to have her rest her foot and perhaps recover. We thought while it was still early in the morning (approximately around 8 am), one of us could go forward to scout the area, in case we were close to the Swaziland border, while one would remain taking care of Monica.

Our dilemma now was to decide who would be the best person for the job. It had to be the person who could speak the dialect of the local people, or at least understands it, so as to minimize the possibility of being identified as a South African on the run. Joel spoke isi-Pedi, which is quite different from the Swati dialect. I was the only person who could do the job.

Although I spoke isi-Xhosa, my dialect was close enough to isi-Swati, the language spoken by the people in the area. I could understand it and at least communicate at a basic level without raising suspicion. Yes, I was more than qualified for the scouting job, and Ahayah had me covered.

I was beaming with confidence and boldness, for I was convinced by now that He was guiding us through this journey. His visitation in my dream was a confirmation that all along, **HE HAD US UNDER HIS WINGS**. I recalled what my father often told me to do, "Always read and pray Psalm 91; you will see your way through." I had not memorized the whole Psalm, but I could remember two verses very well, Psalm 91: verses 4 and 5, which I quietly prayed. I then told my friends that I was fit for the job I would go and come back with good news.

CHAPTER 5
FINDING THE WAY TO "FREEDOM"

Risking life to find "freedom."

Leaving my comrades behind, I went filled with zeal to clear the way that would finally lead us to **"FREEDOM**." The big question is, what is freedom? The Oxford Dictionary defines freedom as "the power or right to act, speak, or think as one wants; absence of subjection to foreign domination or despotic government; the state of not being imprisoned or enslaved."

Well! "state of being imprisoned" can be spiritual, mental, or physical, and it can also be subjective and defined by one's perception of his or her status quo. An example of spiritual imprisonment is that of a king living in a palace, making laws that control all his subjects, while he is spiritually tormented and enslaved by his own state of being.

The scriptures in 1 Samuel 18:10-11) give an account of the life of King Saul, who was tormented and enslaved by an evil spirit;

and became jealous of a shepherd boy named David, such that he sought at all cost to destroy him.

And it came to pass on the morrow, that an evil spirit from The Most High came mightily upon Saul, and he prophesied in the midst of the house: and David played with his hand, as at other times: and there was a javelin in Saul's hand. And Saul cast the javelin; for he said, I will smite David even to the wall with it. And David avoided out of his presence twice. (1Samuel 18:10-11; KJV)

On the other hand, freedom can be experienced in a situation where people are physically imprisoned. The Book of Acts gives an account of how, during the persecution and killings of followers of Christ, His Apostles, such as Paul and Silas, would rejoice and even turn the torture events into opportunities for praising The Most High God while they were in chains.

Although they were physically incarcerated in prison, yet in their mind and spirit, they had freedom through faith in Christ and trust in their Creator's power and His love for them. Their worship and trusting Ahayah resulted in their release from prison, thus obtaining physical freedom. (Acts 16: 23 – 36)

At times, these early Apostles, for the sake of their desire to do Ahayah's will, fought hard through prayers to obtain physical freedom for the sake of preaching the gospel. In the case of Apostle Peter, who was imprisoned, the believers in Christ gathered to intercede for him until an angel was released from heaven to go and open the prison doors for him, so he was able to walk to freedom. (Acts 12: 5-11).

The desire to attain freedom has always been a strong internal goal for which people would strive. The discomforts of life often trigger this desire, driving determined men and women to go to any length to be free from pain. Yes, great men and women have risked their lives, and many others have been martyred while they were on their quest for freedom. Referring to freedom, Nelson Mandela uttered these words:

"........ I have cherished the ideal of a democratic and free society in which all persons live together in harmony and with equal opportunities. It is an ideal that I hope to live for and to achieve. But if needs be, it is an ideal for which I am prepared to die."

Before his assassination, Martin Luther King Jr said these words concerning freedom:

"When we let freedom ring, when we let it ring from every tenement and every hamlet, from every state and every city, we will be able to speed up that day when all of God's children, black men, and white men, Jews, and Gentiles, Protestants, and Catholics, will be able to join hands and sing in the words of the old spiritual, "Free at last, free at last. Thank God Almighty, we are free at last."

As I walked away from the cave, I felt this strong drive to obtain freedom for my two friends and me. Since I had a long way to go to get close to the border fence, I found myself debating in my mind about freedom, what it is and why this strong desire to obtain it. Were we really going to be free?

Nevertheless, what would all that have to do with my friends and I risking our lives to this extent just to be free from oppression, glorified slavery, and discrimination under the Apartheid regime?

WHAT IS FREEDOM?

I wondered what freedom means to The Most High God, whom I later got to know by His real Name: I AM THAT I AM (Ahayah Ashar Ahayah: old Hebrew translation) from reading Exodus 3: 14.

Well, come to think of it, in His original creation, The Most High made man to live freely, covered by His Glory. Man was not bound by sin; he experienced no fear; he was without struggles, without sickness, and without pain. Adam and his wife Eve lived in abundance, lacking nothing while they were still in the garden of Eden, for Ahayah had prepared everything men would need before He created them, male and female (Genesis 1:28-30). They were also given by Him authority to rule and have dominion over all of creation.

And Ahayah blessed them: and Ahayah said unto them, Be fruitful, and multiply, and replenish the earth, and subdue it; and have dominion over the fish of the sea, and over the fowl of the air, and over every living thing that moveth upon the earth. (Gen. 1:28; KJV)

However, as soon as the first man and woman disobeyed The Most High, they lost their privileges and freedom; and were evicted from the garden where there was abundance and safety. Note, the key word here is **DISOBEDIENCE**. Could this mean that there was a **LAW** or **COMMANDMENT** Adam and Eve violated, which resulted in their loss of freedom? It is logical that whenever there are laws and commandments to obey, there must be a Kingdom, a King, and subjects of the Kingdom. The subjects must also have knowledge and understanding of the Kingdom's laws and commandments and willingness to totally submit to the King, thus guaranteeing life, freedom, and access to the King's treasures.

Indeed, Adam and Eve were free to love and worship the only God or High Power they knew, The Most High, the King of the Kingdom of Heaven. They were free to rule over all creation; they enjoyed the service of the angels, the ministering spirits who were commanded to serve them (Hebrews 1:14). They had access to all the herbs, vegetables, and fruits.

The Most High (King) had planted for this family (Genesis 2: 8-9). However, as soon as another king showed up and convinced them to rebel against The King of Heaven by willingly violating the Law which was given to them, Adam and Eve became the subjects of the lesser King, Lucifer.

Nevertheless, Ahayah, The Most High, was not taken by surprise when in Genesis 2:17, His family of men had failed to keep the one Law given to them, which led to their fall from FREEDOM into BONDAGE. He had already prepared His only begotten Son, Yashaya Christ, as the sacrificial Lamb to restore mankind back to the original state from which he had fallen.

And all that dwell upon the earth shall worship him, whose names are not written in the book of life of the Lamb slain from the foundation of the world. (Revelation 13:8; KJV)

Men could regain their FREEDOM only through their belief in His Son, Christ Yashaya, who became a perfect role model through total obedience to His Father. He would redeem and reinstate mankind as the righteousness of The Most High God, worthy to regain and enjoy the lifestyle Ahayah had originally prepared for them.

Obviously, these thoughts were not the kind of mental debate I could entertain at the time, I must admit. Although I was born and grew up in a church environment, my father being a minister of the gospel, as a young adult at the time, I had not diligently studied the Word of The Most High, Ahayah.

Regardless, it is common knowledge that everyone on earth originally descended from Adam and Eve, the original violators of The Most High's Law. This being the case, how is it that today the Negroes or Abantu have become the identifiable group on a large scale on earth, who seem to have totally lost everything our ancestors Adam and Eve enjoyed in the Garden of Eden? Who, then, are these people? Are there special laws they have violated to deserve this level of treatment from all other races? This question and possible explanation will be revisited later in this book.

SCOUTING THE PATH TO A "FREE WORLD"

Well! I felt charged with excitement as I walked through the open graze field that seemed to stretch endlessly. I was full of anticipation of good experiences to come, the very thought of living freely without being discriminated, harassed, and treated like a third-class citizen. Having the opportunity to travel out of the country meant a lot for a South African Bantu those days. It was equated to gaining a degree of superiority and freedom.

You may or may not know that under the Apartheid regime, Bantus were as a race deemed legally inferior and far fewer humans than all other races that were part of the South African Communities, particularly the people of Caucasian descent. We could not be issued a South African passport because we were not legally considered South African citizens. As such, this was to be the first opportunity for me to travel out of South Africa.

As I was drifting through these thoughts, I saw a man walking in my direction. I was, for a moment, hesitant, gripped with fear. Different thoughts were competing in my mind, such as; am I safe; will he blow a whistle on me if he makes demands I cannot fulfill; even if I scream, who is going to hear and rescue me?

My faith was again shaken, yes, me, the very person who had a comforting vision the previous night from an Angel's visitation. As he was coming closer, I began to feel stillness and hope that somehow Ahayah would use him in my favor.

I picked up my pace, enthusiastically walking towards him. I greeted him with my basic isi-Swati, trying to hide my strong isi-Xhosa accent. I wondered why this man did not come from the border gate direction, which was now visible but at a distance. I casually asked him if there was a way through the fence ahead. He responded in his language, "Oh! Yeah, there is a path here through this way; the barbed wire fence is down. People go back and forth through this path all the time".

I thanked him and pretended as if I was going forward toward the fence. As soon as he disappeared from my sight, I turned around and tried to find my way back to where my friends were waiting. It was just before sunset by the time I arrived at the cave. I found them panicking and thinking that I had been caught by the police. They were already making plans to move out of the cave to find another way of escape.

A little angel as a final guide

We made haste to the border fence path, an approximately half-a-day journey that took us only about three or four hours. Monica's ankle had somewhat gotten better. I thanked The Most High! that she had no fracture.

As we were getting closer to the fence, a young boy (he could have been about nine or ten years old) appeared coming towards us. We were not sure of where he appeared from and where he was going at that time of the evening. We asked him how safe it could be for us to cross the fence.

He pointed at the border gate and said: "do you see those white South African soldiers? They are going to start drinking anytime now and get drunk. As soon as they start making noise and singing, you must know that they are drunk; that is your good opportunity to jump the fence." The boy asked for some money, we gave him all the money we had, eight Rands, and he walked away and disappeared.

We sat down, still amazed about what had just happened. It wasn't too long before we could hear the noise and singing of the drunk South African soldiers. We wasted no time and made haste toward the border fence. We safely crossed with the help of the bright moonlight.

This was the best time to cross because the border gate was closed, and most of the Swazi workers would have probably gone off duty. The additional advantage was the obvious observation that this area did not seem to be patrolled by the South African soldiers, which made it relatively safe.

We then walked towards the road on the Swaziland territory that goes towards the border gate. We were fortunate to get a ride from a man who was driving to a small town, an hour's drive from the border. He asked us where we were going. I told him that we belonged to a Catholic Youth Association and that we were going to Mbabane (the Swaziland major city) to a Catholic Youth conference. He apologized that he could only take us as far as the small town because he was now going home. He told us that there was a Catholic Mission convent in town, and he offered to take us to the place to spend the night there so we could proceed the next day.

On our arrival at the Catholic convent, we were warmly welcomed by the Catholic Nuns. By this time, we had not had a meal nor bath for two days, let alone a bed and a pillow to rest our bodies. Nevertheless, we breathed a sigh of relief to have made it out of South Africa without being caught after almost three weeks on the road. More exciting for Monica and me was that this was our first experience of being out of the country in which we were born. We were served a warm, full meal.

We bathed and were given comfortable beds for the night. The next morning, we were offered a ride to Mbabane by the unsuspecting Catholic Nuns after a good breakfast.

CHAPTER 6
TESTING THE MOMENTS OF "FREEDOM"

Although we enjoyed our free movements in Mbabane, we did not want to lose focus; our goal was to move quickly close to our destiny, Mozambique. After all, being in Swaziland was not completely safe; we knew it was the backyard of South African undercover police.

We were now exhausted and were not prepared to undertake another long unknown trip on foot. We needed money. I decided to close an account I had with a major bank that had a branch in Swaziland. I withdrew whatever was available, 20 Rands (approximately $2). This amount was enough to at least pay for our public transport fare to the next town, Manzini.

I was already feeling homesick, missing both my parents and my two beautiful girls. Before we took the bus to Manzini, I quickly sent a telegram (telegraphic wire message) to my parents, informing them of my whereabouts. Oh! I was so naïve and inexperienced to think my communication with my parents would be private when the police knew I was 'on the run. Yes, little did I know that my telegraphic was going to be intercepted by the South African police, thereby giving them a lead.

In addition, while I was testing the moments of my freedom by freely sending this message, I had put my parents in danger. I later learned that as a result of my message, my parents were harshly interrogated by the police, who wanted to know my whereabouts and what they knew regarding my political activities.

THE NAÏVE BUNCH

When we arrived in Manzini, we quickly got another bus to Siteki, a town close to the Lomahasha border gate leading to Mozambique. We arrived in Siteki just before sunset. We had hoped to make it to the border of Swaziland and Mozambique that same day. We approached a man who was on his way home after his day's work to direct us to the border gate. He informed us that it would take a long walking distance to get there, and the border gate was already closed.

This man, who introduced himself as Dlamini, kindly invited us to his village home so we could spend a night with his family. On arrival at his home, we were welcomed by his hospitable wife, Thembi, who served us tea and biscuits.

Before we settled for the evening, we freely told the family who we were and the purpose of our journey. The family sympathized with our course, but they were surprised by our boldness of planning to go through the Swaziland border without passports.

They knew what we did not know, Swaziland government officials at the time were working together with a South African police agency. In fact, we got to learn that Thembi's brother, who lived with the family, worked at the Lomahasha border as one of the officers. He had seen several South African refugees getting detained by the Swazi government and got sent back to South Africa.

Clearly, we were the naïve bunch that had no clue about the political dynamics of the Southern African region. All we knew was how badly the Apartheid laws of the South African government were affecting us and how we were determined to go and fight for our freedom and that of our people. We were also convinced that beyond our South African fenced borders, we would be free and safe.

STRATEGIC CROSSING

Shortly after our evening meal Dlamini and his wife Thembi asked how we got to Siteki from South Africa and how we managed to cross the border to Swaziland. We trusted them enough to roll out the narrative tape about our adventurous and dangerous trip. While we were still giving them the account of our journey, Thembi's brother Moses, who worked at the border gate, arrived.

After listening to our story and the plan to cross over to Mozambique, Moses offered to help us. He informed us that one of the evening officers who guard the border gate was always quick to inform the South African police whenever refugees tried to cross the border. Moses suggested that he would go ahead in the morning and make certain that the night shift officers were gone off duty. He would then call his sister through their family landline (there were no cell phones then) and ask her to show us directions that would safely take us to the border.

Border Drama

Moses' arrangement went well. When we arrived at the border, he kept his colleague busy and signaled for us to quickly go through without stopping to talk to them. We moved quickly without looking back. It was a long stretch of land between the two borders. Suddenly we heard chaotic noise behind us, one officer called to have us return to the border, and we ignored him. We heard a sound of an army jeep arriving; we looked back and saw two white South African soldiers who were probably notified about us crossing the border.

It wasn't long before we heard the sound of gunshots, but by this time, we were running very fast without looking back. As we ran forward, we saw two Mozambique soldiers coming towards us with guns, ready to shoot. We froze, not knowing the direction to which we should run. Joel shouted, "Let's go forward; we are better off facing the Mozambique soldiers than the Boers" (Boers, a South African term used to identify Caucasians of Dutch descendant).

Surely, it was safer running towards them regardless of what would be awaiting us ahead. After all, we had come too far to turn back and surrender to the South African or Swaziland authorities, which would lead to facing torture and/or death. Nevertheless, we narrowly escaped the South African bullets! Indeed! He (Ahayah) had covered us with His feathers, and under His wings, Ahayah gave us refuge (Psalm 91:4).

CHAPTER 7
LIFE IN THE "FREE WORLD" BEGINS

Barracks experience

Meeting friendly and unthreatening soldiers was not only a great relief but also an unusual experience for us. The Mozambique soldiers kept us in their border barracks for about a week. Communication with the soldiers was proving to be a struggle. They spoke only Portuguese language and other African languages we could not understand. We all resorted to make-do sign language and some broken English.

Monica and I felt somewhat uncomfortable sharing rooms and bathrooms with men we did not know, particularly soldiers whose job had obviously separated them from their families. Each day she and I kept close watch of each other, shared the same blanket at bedtime and held onto each other until daybreak. Joel appeared to be oblivious to our fears as he blended well with the guys.

Hope for "Freedom"

An arrangement was made for us to be transported to Maputo, the capital city of Mozambique. On the morning of the fifth day of our stay at the Mozambique border, shortly after we had breakfast, an army jeep with two soldiers arrived from Maputo to transport us.

We were quite excited about our new life ahead of us in a "free" country. Monica and I had built many castles in the air about how glorious our lives were going to be. Joel, on the other hand, seemed to have one thing on his mind – training to be a soldier and go back to South Africa to fight for freedom.

We did not let him into our world because he believed we had the same plans as his. I knew I was too much of a coward to be a soldier; that was definitely not my plan. I only looked forward to living a "free" life, like the one (in my perception) that was being enjoyed by our fellow "White" South Africans. The freedom to work and live where ever I wished and be paid a salary based on my education and experience, not based on my race or the color of my skin. That was my definition of free life. That was what I was hoping to attain and enjoy in Mozambique. What a narrow view of freedom!

Who was really free in South Africa? Looking back now and having spoken with some of the Caucasian South Africans with whom I later became acquainted, no one seemed to be totally free. Everybody lived under the demonic spell of HATRED, FEAR and PARANOIA that caused indescribable PAIN.

COULD THIS BE OUR DREAM REALIZED?

We travelled to Maputo with the two soldiers for several hours. The trip seemed quite long, perhaps for several reasons. First, there was little or no communication between the soldiers and us due to the language barrier. Even if we could try, it would be difficult because the ride was rather rough, noisy and bumpy, such that we had to hold tight onto this army vehicle that had no top cover.

Second, we were so excited about the prospect of finally getting to our "DREAMLAND", our sort-after destination. We knew we would be envied by the friends we left behind in South Africa for having made it. We thought this was indeed "A dream that was coming through" in the true sense. We couldn't wait to get to Maputo.

Thirdly, as the morning was handing over to midday, the heat of the tropical sun was gaining its strength. Nevertheless, this was the least of our concerns, minimized by our anticipation of a better life and big dreams.

From Barracks To Upgrade Barracks

We arrived in Maputo, the major city of Mozambique, just before 2 pm. We were taken to Jardim, an apartment building that housed the Frelimo private soldiers (Jardim - means garden, close to Botanical gardens) who worked at the offices of the Frelimo Head Quarters. Frelimo was the movement, led by

President Samora Machel, that fought for the liberation of Mozambique from the colonial rule of the Portuguese.

We arrived in Jardim at the time the soldiers were getting ready to return to work after their two-hour lunch break. We received a warm welcome, and we were taken to our rooms after being served a delicious seafood meal. Monica and I shared one bedroom, and Joel had his own room. We lived in these "glorified barracks" for three months. Throughout this period, no government official or anybody sat us down and asked about our plans. I believed we were being observed to see if we would be a security threat.

The Kidnap Drama

At the beginning of the second month, Joel became restless and asked to be taken to where he could receive military training. He made it clear that he was not there to idle but to achieve what he had come to do in Mozambique, train and go back to South Africa to fight. He asked us to join him as he had it in his mind that we had the same goals, but we refused to go with him.

At the end of that week, two soldiers arrived in an army jeep and forcefully took Monica and I to army barracks where Joel was receiving training. This happened while all the Jardim residents were at work. This was one of the terrifying experiences, particularly when we suddenly found ourselves in a barracks full of all-men soldiers. Joel confessed that he was responsible for this drama.

He told them that training to be soldiers was the purpose of our coming to Mozambique and that he was not happy that we had changed our plans.

Escape Plan

Monica and I could not imagine spending even one night at these barracks. It was too overwhelming, to say the least. We asked ourselves many questions with no answers. What was our future going to look like? What about our plans? Is this the beginning of the end of our lives? I personally associated a soldier's lifestyle with a short life span.

I was purely a coward and was not prepared to choose a fast lane to my grave. Besides, we could have been raped by these soldiers. I was imagining the worst and could not see myself staying even for one night at this place. We had to come up with a brilliant plan, a quick one that would save us from having to spend a night.

We knew that trying to escape would be foolish and dangerous. We then went to see one of the commanders and explained that we had left all our belongings behind and, most importantly, our underwear and feminine necessities. We explained that we were not informed that we were coming for training. We requested to be taken back to only fetch our belongings so we would be well prepared for the training.

Our plan worked. One unassuming soldier was sent to drive us back to Jardim so we could fetch our belongings as we had requested.

On our arrival, we quickly went to report to the officials, who by this time had returned from the Frelimo Head Quarters after their day's work. We were protected, and the soldier was told to return to the barracks.

SUBMITTING TO MAN'S PROTECTION

Monica and I began to wonder if another attempt would be made to have us back at the training camp without any further protection. We felt insecure, not knowing what would happen next. Two of the male Frelimo officers who also lived on the same floor with us began to take a personal interest in us.

At first, we thought these two men were only helping us to learn the Portuguese language in preparation for when we would be given our own accommodation and begin to live our normal lives. It did not take long before we caught on and understood that they were intimately attracted to us. Well, at this point, we felt quite vulnerable and in need of some form of protection.

We began to reason that we needed assurance in knowing that we would be protected and that these men would help us get settled in this foreign country. After all, they were good-looking, kind men who appeared to have some influence and a degree of authority.

In fact, we had approached one of them when we needed protection from the barracks soldiers. We decided to get involved and quickly fell in love with them.

A month later, in this relationship, I realized that I had conceived and shared this news with "my man". I began to notice restlessness in him. At this point, he appeared to be quite close and committed to the relationship. He started thinking and talking about how I could be taken to his family. He showed me his sister's photos.

However, there was much fear written all over his face and a sense of panic, as if he did not know what to do and how to go about accomplishing his desire. Monica's boyfriend, who could speak more clearly in English, began to explain that his friend could be severely punished if the top senior officials got to know about this matter and that if it was up to him, he would take me to his home.

Well, two weeks later, our comfortable stay with these Frelimo officials suddenly came to an end. It felt like a rooftop was blown away by a windy storm and left us unprotected. Yes, we did not trust in the Lord but in our own understanding. Had I focused on seeking Ahayah's plan and wisdom, I would have perhaps remembered His counsel in Proverbs 3:5;

"Trust in The Lord with all your heart, And lean not on your own understanding".

A number of concerning thoughts began to compete in my mind: what does the future hold for me and my unborn child? ; will I ever again see the father of this child? How am I going to survive in a foreign country with an infant? Have I allowed fears of the unknown and insecurities to replace my dreams? Did I shut Ahayah out of the process of attaining my dreams? Did I ever consider Ahayah's plans for my life and purposed to pursue them in the first place?

What about the freedom of my nation? How was I to contribute now to attain that part of my dream? Needless to say, I had many questions with no answers. I felt I had failed The Lord, myself, my parents, and the people I had left behind struggling under the iron hand of the Apartheid regime.

CHAPTER 8
CHANGING HANDS

It was in December 1975, three months after we had arrived in Maputo, when the Frelimo officials handed us over to the United Nations High Commissioner for Refugees (UNHCR). Monica and I were moved to the UNHCR house. We found other refugees from different countries, including four other South Africans. 'This is a good deal! we thought; they are finally convinced that we do not have what it takes for one to be a soldier.' We began to dream again; the possibilities of furthering our education and living "freely" could be a reality.

The refugees who had been accommodated in the UNHCR house seemed to be well informed about our rights and how well we would be protected under the care of the UNHCR. It was a comfortable homely environment where visions and aspirations could possibly be entertained and attained by fellow refugees. Everyone seemed to be relaxed and content with life.

There seemed to be no reason to worry about what tomorrow would or would not bring.

We were served daily with three good meals and snacks in between meals. For a people without a vision, this was a "perfect lifestyle"; after all, what more would anyone want?

A man without a vision perishes!

Nevertheless, three of the four South Africans we found in the house were different from the rest of the refugees. They wanted more than just free meals and comfortable beds. They seemed to have understood Ahayah's warning that:

"Where there is no vision, the people perish; but he that keepeth the law, happy is he." (Proverbs 29:18. KJV)

These South Africans had thoroughly researched various supports one could receive from the UNHCR and the available scholarships for people who wanted to pursue tertiary education. Surely, they seemed to be our God-sent guide to get us to the path of our dreams.

Two of these South Africans were a married couple, Musa and Miriam, and were Christians, although they missed one thing, they did not completely keep the laws and commandments of The Most High, as written in Exodus 20, verses 1 to 17. The name of the third South African was John. This couple kept talking about the faithfulness of God and how He was able to bring our dreams to fruition.

I was not ready to fully admit that I understood their way of thinking due to my guilt about what I had done at the Jardin.

Although no one knew about my pregnancy at that point, except for Monica, since I was still in my first trimester, I was wearing a garment of guilt and shame; I was nursing my emotional wounds. This couple was talking about the very Most High Power who, earlier on our journey, had proved Himself to be faithful enough to see us through the two borders of Swaziland under His Wings.

This couple's strong faith in God encouraged Monica and me to seriously explore the possibilities of moving on to other countries through the help of the UNHCR to fulfill our dreams. We visited the UNHCR office and affirmed that we were on the right path. Finally! We were now convinced that our dreams would possibly come through. We were determined not to perish in Mozambique.

Often time when we are in our comfort zones, we can take life for granted. We assume that as we go to sleep in our warm and comfortable beds, we will wake up and go about our business as usual. The reality is that we do not make decisions about our life span, nor can we really tell outside our human plans what might happen from moment to moment of our lives. While at times we are aware of this truth, it is often kept at the subconscious level of our minds or perhaps not even considered as important during our robust time of youth. In coming to grip with this truth, David recalled in Psalm 102: 11 that:

"My days are like a shadow that declineth; and I am withered like grass." (KJV)

King David said this in recognition of the short span of men, and yet Ahayah cares and values each life He has created. Yes,

He does! He also desires that men seek Him and get to know and pursue the purpose for which he or she was created. He has also promised that no matter what happens, He is committed to never leave or forsake those who love Him and keep His laws and commandments.

The Chaotic Move!

The hopes were high; all was good and proper but short-lived when our lives were disrupted by a sudden "chaotic move." It was early on a beautiful morning in January 1976; the sun was just emerging from its "resting place" when we were woken and startled by chaotic noise. A bus with a large enough number of soldiers to resurface the unpleasant memories of barracks early experience had stopped in front of our resident house. Some of the soldiers stormed into the house and forcefully ordered us to quickly pack our belongings and board the bus.

Two soldiers forcefully dragged Miriam into a vehicle without offering any reason for their actions. Musa tried to protect his wife as he attempted to pull her back, releasing her from one of the soldier's hands. They threatened to shoot him if he continued to interfere with their operation.

There were screams and indescribable chaos all around, and people were feeling confused, scared, and uncertain of what was to happen next. The two soldiers quickly drove away with Miriam. Musa was left behind, very disturbed, and frantically asked some of the soldiers who came with the bus the reason for his wife's kidnap by the soldiers.

While all this was going on, the soldiers forced all of us, the refugees, to quickly board the bus. They were intimidating, holding big guns (known as Bazookas) as if they could shoot anyone who would resist. Two soldiers, on the other hand, were charging at Musa, threatening to shoot him as he was getting angry, refusing to board the bus without his wife. Finally, the bus pulled off with all of us packed in, uninformed about the destination.

Dreams aborted

We travelled, undertaking a day's journey, during which we made a few bathroom stops. We finally arrived at a small town called Chai-Chai at the end of that day, close to about six in the early evening. The soldiers informed us that the move to this small town was for our protection because it would have been dangerous for us as refugees to continue living in the big city.

Needless to mention that this sudden move to a rather remote area of the country was unsettling, particularly to John, Monica, and me. We felt that our plan to pursue education in any of the English-speaking countries through the help of the UNHCR had been aborted. We had already initiated this process by making our plans known to the UNHCR and requesting them to assist us.

We had not yet received any response when we left the capital city of Maputo, where we thought our dreams and hopes were eventually going to be realized. Nevertheless, we were now mostly preoccupied and worried about Miriam's arrest. We also tried to provide emotional support to Musa, although no one could think of any solution.

Venturing into the woods

It had been two weeks long since we had arrived in Chai-chai, a remote small town we had come to believe was going to be our new home, at least for a while. Just as we were beginning to settle down and becoming comfortable, sleeping and waking up purposelessly, another sudden change was imposed on us.

We had hardly finished our breakfast meal when on a Sunday morning, a convoy of army jeeps arrived and stopped in front of the building in which we were accommodated. We were again commanded to quickly collect our belongings and get into these jeeps. This should not have surprised us, but believe me, we were all shocked and confused by this sudden move. This is because we had somehow gotten information from "the grapevine" that Chai-chai was our destination.

Nevertheless, we knew the drill! As such, we were ready in no time, which was not surprising since we were already trained to respond quickly without hesitation to the soldiers' commands. Not one of us would dare ask why we were being moved and where our new destination was going to be.

Wilderness, our new home!

We hopped onto the jeeps and embarked on another whole day's journey to a new world. At about nine at night, we arrived at a place that was very dark and looked like a forest. We were told to quickly find wood and make a fire in order to keep off wild animals. With the help of the vehicle's headlights, we managed to find woods and made a fire under a huge tree, where we all set and waited for the dawn of a new day.

Here we were nervously keeping a big fire burning throughout the night to ward off animals – what animals, lions? Bears? Maybe cobras? Who knows. Where was our faith in our God, who had demonstrated His care for us and ability to protect us on our journey from South Africa to this point? Yet our Most High God had already given us the promise of His protection in Psalm 91verses 8 and 13.

Mhhh! I wondered if these verses were written for me for such a time as this. Oh! Talking of adders or snakes, It didn't take long before I got the answer to that question. My friend Monica had fallen asleep next to the fire when a big poisonous snake dropped from a huge tree under which we were seated and hit her head. It was a female cobra who had her babies up on the tree. The babies, who were also quite large, followed and dropped down.

This big fall stirred up quite a scare that caused all of us to jump and scatter in different directions. The soldiers who were already sleeping in their jeeps quickly woke up and turned on the vehicle lights for us to scan the area. The snakes had disappeared into the bush; probably, they were also scared.

As we settled down around the fire, I prayed hard for the dawn to come sooner than its normal time of appearance. The thought of getting a snake bite, and of all places, in such a remote area where medical help is only a luxurious dream, was unbearable. It would certainly mean death and burial in the bush, and my family would have never known when and how my life ended. A scary thought.

CHAPTER 9
THE WOODS LIFE EXPERIENCE

Life in "Casa da Morte"

Even though I walk through the valley of the shadow of death, I shall fear no evil for you are with me. Your rod and your stuff they comfort me" (Psalm 23).

It was in the summer month of February 1976 when we arrived in this forestry-like wilderness, a place we later referred to as "Casa da Morte" and to be suitably translated as "Death Camp." We only used the name to express how we felt about our experience living in the place. Well! Following the cobra's debut, the soldiers instructed us to cut down trees and quickly build wooden shacks for them. We were ordered and followed at gunpoint to carry out this hard labour.

It was about four on a summer morning, and the light of the dawning day had started to appear. As the sun slowly appeared, we began to see the layout of the place and were able to start the construction with our bare hands. My three friends and I quickly formed a team as we tried to make sense of the rather difficult unimaginable task we were to accomplish.

The soldiers who watched us labour began to mock us, saying, "You South Africans are used to big cities. Now build a city right here and make a home for yourselves. "We made haste to build the soldiers' shelters and completed two sizable wooden houses by early afternoon. We quickly started working on our shelters. We were all highly motivated and determined to complete two more buildings before it became dark. We had to avoid the previous night's experience of sitting all night around a fire. We also feared the unknown.

By evening we had completed two other small cabins made from tree branches. We were just under thirty refugees in all, Monica and I being the only females. We all squeezed into these shacks, feeling very proud of our accomplishments.

Diet in Casa da Morte

As the environment changed from urban Maputo's comfortable lifestyle to the bushy wilderness camp, so was our diet. Our meals were simple and basic, consisting of maize (corn) meal porridge with sugar for breakfast and thick maize meal porridge (pap) served with sugar beans for lunch/dinner. These were our two daily meals.

A small pond of stagnant water nearby, covered with green algae, served as our only source of water for cooking, drinking, and washing. Although we tried to purify the water for drinking by boiling it, a few of us were already suffering from dysentery from drinking the water by the end of the second week. However, The Most High kept me and my friends healthy, surviving the worst living condition we had ever experienced; why? Did Yashaya Christ not say in Mark 16:

...... And these signs shall follow them that believe; In my Name .... verse 18: They shall take up serpents; and if they drink any deadly thing, it shall not hurt them; .... (Mark 16: verses16 to 18. KJV)

Well! Truth be told, my friends John, Monica, and I did not deserve this protection since we did not meet the requirements according to these scripture verses. I believe we were covered by The Most High's grace because He had better plans for us which had to be fulfilled; Musa, by his admission, met these requirements; I also believe that my parents had not stopped interceding for me and for my protection. Therefore, dying in this wilderness camp could not be our lot by any stretch of imagination.

Strategic Escape Plan

Summer months in Mozambique often had heavy rains and floods, particularly in the month of February. Towards the end of our second week at the camp, the heavy rains had already started to fall. We were all, including the soldiers, getting tired of our monotonous diet without any vegetables, meat, or fish. Musa, who was still distraught and determined to find his wife's whereabouts, came up with a brilliant idea of how we could escape from the camp.

We were to sell the idea of forming teams that could take turns and go fishing from the small ponds a little further away from the camp. It was generally known that when the heavy rains fell, fish would often be found in ponds, interestingly, except for the one next to the camp with algae. This idea was well received by the soldiers. They had also started to relax and had eased off from keeping a close check on us.

We proposed to form teams of three people. Our plan was to have Musa, John, and I form a team that would be the first to go fishing.

We decided to exclude Monica from the plan. We reasoned that because Monica was of mixed race (classified as colored in South Africa), going with her would probably raise suspicion and cause us to be easily identified as foreigners. We feared that we could be caught, arrested, or killed before we could get to Maputo and accomplish our purpose.

We also reasoned that Monica would probably not survive the journey because of her slightly heavy weight. I was emotionally torn between advocating for my close friend Monica to be included in our team and letting go for the purpose of our most important goal, to find Musa's wife.

My personal struggle was that I had come to know and trust Monica more than these two men with whom I was to embark yet on another dangerous journey. I was also troubled by the thought of leaving her behind, the only female, with all these strange men. However, I also knew that Monica might indeed not survive another unknown long and potentially dangerous trip due to her once-injured ankle. After quietly weighing all these pros and cons, I decided to keep her out of our secret plan.

CHAPTER 10
THE FISHING TRIP OF NO RETURN

"I will go before thee and make the crooked places straight; I will break in pieces the gates of brass and cut in sunder the bars of iron."

(Isaiah 45:2; King James Version).

Early on a Monday morning, at about four o'clock, just before the dawn took over from the dusk, Musa, John, and I freely left the camp, leaving everyone with hopes that we were coming back with fish that was to be prepared for breakfast. Interestingly, no one asked how we were going to fish without fishing equipment. I suppose it was assumed that we would just catch the fish with our bare hands, wrap it live with our clothing, and bring it back to the camp.

Since it seemed none of us had the fishing experience anyway (including the soldiers), no one had the smarts to think of asking such a question. The soldiers probably trusted that, being South

Africans, we could be experienced fishers, which could be one of the reasons they did not bother to ask.

We began walking in the last darkest hour of the morning without knowing the direction or having a sense of how we were going to get to Maputo. We did not know where we were geographically positioned, the name of the area where the wilderness camp was, nor did we have any clue of the distance we were to travel ahead of us. We were so driven and determined to leave the camp that it would not have mattered much anyway, even if we were well informed.

We went past a stream of water not very far from the camp, where we could have done our fishing. We then began our long walk on open fields that were sandy and very slushy from the rain, which made it hard to walk fast. There was not a single soul on our path, nor did we see any village or community dwellings. It felt like we were walking across a desert or perhaps tasting a bit of the wilderness journey that the Israelites undertook from Egypt, led by Moses, which is documented in the book of Exodus.

One may recall how The Most High delivered our forefathers, the descendants of Israel from Egypt, leading them through the wilderness after the miracle crossing of the Reed (Red) Sea experience. Indeed, we felt we had just been delivered from Casa da Morte, where life seemed to have no purpose.

As the day progressed, and the tropical sun also gained its strength, we felt hungry, thirsty, and slowing down. We spotted bushes that had wild fruit. We picked the fruit, prayed over it, and trusted Ahayah's protection that it would not harm us. We walked throughout that day without running into a single soul, nor did we see any villages or livestock.

It started to get dark, and we were completely exhausted. The sandy grounds were damp from the heavy rains, even after the scorch of the sunny day. We had no choice but to rest by squatting on the grass and sometimes kneeling to avoid getting wet. We made it through the night and greeted the dawn with enthusiasm.

Day two, a day of miracles!: "What took you so long...?"

As we proceeded to walk, we saw at a distance a Negro (black) woman who was hawing in a field. When she saw us, she immediately threw the haw down and ran to meet us. Before she could greet, she said, "what took you so long? I have been waiting for you all morning. The Lord informed me that you were coming. Come, let me prepare something for you to eat."

She took us to a small patch of land which had a shack that was in the middle of nowhere. This place was not too far from where she was hawing. In front of this shack, there was a shelter made with four poles and covered only on the top to make a comfortable shade. She had a beautiful traditional African mat laid under this shelter. She asked us to sit down and rest. She then went into the shack and came out with a jar of drinking water that was as cold as the refrigerated water. We drank and satisfied our thirst.

While we still marveled at this whole hospitality and how she could have such cold water in the middle of nowhere without electricity, the woman went back to the shack and came out with three dishes of food that were prepared for us. I have never tasted such a delicious meal before then and up to this day. We ate our fill and drank some more water.

The woman informed us that we still had a very long way to travel as she seemed to know where we were going and instructed us to lie down and rest. She also promised that she would wake us up later to proceed with our journey. In addition, the woman informed us that we were heading towards the North, in the opposite direction from Maputo and that she would give us directions later.

It was approximately 4 o'clock in the afternoon when she woke us up and gave us another meal, after which she showed us a way towards a stream and a path through a patch of dense trees. She informed us that through this dense forestry is an uphill path at the end of which we would find a grocery shop.

She said that on our arrival at this shop, we would find the owner, an East-Indian-looking man who would have just closed his shop and getting ready to drive in his small pickup truck to the next town. This man would give us a ride without asking much about who we were and the purpose of our journey.

We took off and proceeded towards the stream and through the dense trees as directed. We arrived at the shop just as the man was about to get into his van. We got the ride to the next town, which turned out to be an hour's journey. Although the man was going further than the town, we asked him to drop us off and pretended as if we had arrived at our destination.

On arrival at this town, The Most High gave us the wisdom and courage to find a government office that used to be called at the time Sede Partido. We were welcomed by a young man who spoke English fluently and was of mixed race (People of mixed race in Mozambique were identified as Mulatto).

We informed him that we were university students from South Africa and that we were touring the country and admiring its new independence. He was thrilled and offered us hotel accommodation. "Oh, what a great amazing favour!" I quickly said quietly under my breath, "The Most High has done it again!" As King David would say in the book of Psalms:

For thou, Lord, wilt bless the righteous; with favour wilt thou compass him as with a shield (Psalms 5:12. KJV)

The Most High caused us to find favour in the eyes of the government officials and close their eyes such that they would not suspect that we were fugitives on the run.

Day 3: Journey To The Bridge

On this third day of our journey to Maputo, we woke up early, treated ourselves to a warm shower, and headed out at daybreak to the main road, where we were dropped off by the shopkeeper. We began to hitchhike but without success. We were now confident that we were going South toward Maputo. We walked for a good part of the day, getting tired, thirsty, and very hungry. Ahayah, our sustainer, showed up with a solution one more time.

This time we met two boys of about ten or twelve years of age who offered us coconuts. They skillfully broke the coconuts opened and offered us cold water from inside the shells, which just hit the spot. This was my first time ever seeing the original coconut.

You see, I was born in the Eastern Cape Province of South Africa, close to the Maluti mountains, where heavy snow falls during winter times. Although we mostly got frost and wind chill from the mountains, coconut trees and such crops that need a more tropical kind of climate would not do well in the Eastern Cape Province. I was, however, familiar with coconut flakes that came in a packet and were sold in grocery stores. My mother, whose hobby was baking cakes, often used coconut flakes as one of her favorite ingredients.

My friends and I sat down and enjoyed the coconut meal. As we continued on our journey, we also came across wild-grown mango trees along the road that were loaded with mangoes. We were able to harvest and ate a few. We continued to walk on this road that seemed to be hardly traveled by both pedestrians and vehicles.

We reasoned that if we came across any form of transport, we would need some cash to pay our way to our destination. The only asset we had was John's wristwatch that we could sell if we could find a buyer. Ahayah, who knows and gives to His children the desires of their hearts, did not take long before He responded.

While we were thinking and discussing this need, suddenly, we saw a young man who appeared to be going in the opposite direction. We stopped him and tried to sell the watch to him, communicating with a few words we had learned of the local vernacular language.

Surprisingly, the young man was happy to buy the watch at what we considered a good price. We just believed The Most High that whatever we had would be sufficient for the journey ahead of us.

The near-drowning experience.

"Yea, though I walk through the valley of the shadow of death, I will fear no evil, for thou art with me ..... (Psalm 23.4)

It was now about 4 or 5 o'clock in the afternoon when we saw the first vehicle driving on the road, heading in the same direction as us. We were so thrilled and desperate that we would not allow it to pass without stopping for us.

It was a Caucasian man who was driving a pickup van with a canopy. We asked if he could give us a ride to Maputo, and yes, he was indeed going to the same city. He consented, and we hopped in at the back of the van, and he drove off.

It seemed we had traveled for at least two hours before it started to get dark outside. We were not bothered since we knew we would arrive in Maputo that same day. While we were relaxed and thanked The Most High God for His grace, suddenly, we heard a banging noise as if the van had a serious problem. It had stopped awkwardly with the front wheels engaged on a slope. The driver instructed us to slowly and carefully get off the van as he was also so doing.

He was approaching a bridge to drive across the Great Limpopo River. He had not noticed that the floods caused by heavy rain had swept the bridge away, and it was all broken. The Most High had held the vehicle with a cement blog of whatever was left of the bridge, not large enough to logically stop the van from drowning.

I believe the angels held it back to save us from drowning in the big overflowing river. We slowly got out of the van and witnessed the saving hand of the Almighty Ahayah and how He watched His Word to fulfill it. Indeed! He delivered in accordance with His word, (Psalm 91:12)

The Locust Dinner

As we got out of this van, we realized that there was overflowing water all around with small patches of islands. There was also a patch of grass on the other side of the road on which a group of people were standing. They were also traveling but were stuck and could not cross the river. We joined them and spent our third night standing with the group. As the night advanced, people began to feel hungry.

There were locusts jumping everywhere on this grass. A few men collected some of the locusts and got them ready to prepare a meal. One of the men took two stones and rubbed them together very hard to produce fire. Some of the people had already collected wood from the nearby trees.

We made a fire, roasted the locusts, and had dinner. Although I had never had the experience of eating locusts, I did not think twice about it but joined the feast. After all, this was John the Baptist's staple diet. It might have been healthy and sustaining; why not take the chance?

During the night, these Mozambicans began to chant liberation songs until morning. Singing liberation songs was very popular; not surprising it had hardly been a year since the country had regained its independence from Portuguese colonial rule.

Singing songs that acknowledged their leader, President Samora Machel was not only politically correct, but it was also an emotional exercise that expressed their sense of gratitude.

President Machel was a soldier who led the Frelimo Liberation Movement to victory in the war against the Portuguese in1975. He had now become the first President of the country. These Mozambicans appeared to feel quite indebted to this courageous man, as well as to his Liberation Movement comrades, and rightfully so.

Well! We quickly joined in as we had learned the songs while we were at Casa da Morte. It was important for us to blend in with the Mozambicans to avoid being easily identified as fugitives. We had no doubt that there could have been a wild search for us already, probably since the day we left the camp for fishing and did not return. However, thank The Most High that the technology at the time was not as advanced and quick as it is today; otherwise, we probably would have been caught.

In fact, The Most High, through His Spirit, later informed me that He had redirected us to go toward the North for safety because there were soldiers in helicopters who were commanded to find us. They would have easily caught and killed us without mercy had we initially taken the route toward the South. This revelation was later confirmed by my close friend Monica who we had left at the camp.

When I met her years later, she shared that the soldiers interrogated her, asking about our whereabouts. They suspected that we were informers and enemies of the Frelimo. She informed me that helicopters with armed soldiers were released to look for us in the direction of Maputo. However, Ahayah had promised in Psalm 91 verse 11 that He would accompany us and defend us.

Through His grace, we were surely travelling under the wings of The Most High.

At the crack of dawn, we noticed that there were two men who became suspicious of our identity. They began to engage us in conversation, addressing us in both the Portuguese language and one of the local dialects. Musa quickly responded as he could somehow manage one of the local languages while John and I moved closer to those who kept the singing going.

It was clear, though, by his accent, that Musa was not a Mozambican. Besides, our physical features were giving us away; we did not look quite like Mozambicans but clearly like South Africans.

Strategic boat escape

In the early morning, at approximately about seven or eight o'clock, we saw at a distance a motorboat coming in our direction. A Portuguese man who apparently owned a shop across the Great Limpopo River was coming to rescue everybody. As it was getting closer, we noted that the boat could only take four passengers at a time. We quickly positioned ourselves, determined to go on the first trip.

As soon as the boat arrived, we hastily boarded, uninvited, and appeared to have surprised everyone except the boat owner, who seemed to be in a hurry to accomplish his task. One more spot was taken by one of the men who were suspicious. We immediately suspected that he would go and blow the whistle on us as soon as we arrived on the other side of the river.

What he did not know was that throughout this journey, we were traveling under **His Wings.**

Indeed, as soon as we arrived across the river, there was a passenger bus ready to pull off for Maputo. We quickly boarded the bus using the money we got from John's wristwatch sale. Closing the door behind John, who was the last passenger to get in, the bus driver pulled off. We were full of excitement. It was as if the bus had been waiting for us. Ahayah had done it again!

As we looked through the window, we saw the man who was with us in the boat standing and looking quite amazed and disappointed. The shop was still closed, and even if he wanted to make a phone call, he had no access to the facilities. The shop owner had gone back to rescue other people across the river. Well! As the scripture has it:

The wicked watcheth the righteous, and seeketh to slay him. The Lord will not leave him in his hand nor condemn him when he is judged (Psalm 37: 32-33. KJV).

The other interesting miracle was that the money from the watch sale was exactly the amount needed to pay for the three of us to get to Maputo. The Most High was clearly determined to take us to our intended destination and assist us in accomplishing our mission. Primarily, we were desperate to find Monica at all costs.

We also wanted to inform the UNHCR of the events that had taken place since the great move from Maputo.

We arrived in Maputo just before lunchtime. We quickly went to find a mailbox to mail a letter we had written to the United Nations High Commissioner For Refugees, Geneva Headquarters. We wrote to ask for assistance that would enable us to go and pursue education in English-speaking countries. We also reported how Miriam had been taken at gunpoint and that we were requesting the UNHCR to assist us in finding her.

Lastly, we asked if we could be protected such that we wouldn't have to go back to the camp from where we had escaped. We found a post office, purchased the stamp with a few coins Musa had, and mailed the letter. Our first task was accomplished.

We quickly went to the local UNHCR office, where we had been registered as refugees, to report all about what had happened. We had hoped that we would at least get the protection we needed and immediate assistance in finding Miriam.

To our disappointment, the UNHCR commissioner instructed us to go and report ourselves to the government office, which was the headquarters of the Frelimo party. In hearing this, we felt let down and quite betrayed by the very organization we thought would protect us.

I thought, 'what has just happened after all the favors and miraculous protection The Most High gave us throughout our four-days journey under His Wings!.' The problem was that we still looked to men for rescue and protection. It seemed we had not fully taken The Most High God at His Word (Psalm 91: 15).

After all, what is new? We still behaved like our forefathers, the stiff-necked children of Israel who rebelled in the wilderness and did not trust in The God of Israel. They disregarded all the miracles and protection He had shown them in Egypt, including the miraculous Red Sea crossing. Did we even think of calling upon Him? I personally did not even think of it. We were just executing our plan, doing what we thought was logical according to the human mind, particularly to the mind of a refugee who was in trouble.

Although we had enjoyed the evidence of His grace and faithfulness along the way, we had not considered King David's declaration as written in Psalm 91 verse 2. Clearly, we had the unmerited grace through our Lord Yashaya Christ.

Nevertheless, we had no choice but to go and report to the government officials. On our arrival at the Frelimo offices, it seemed they already knew that we were coming. I believe the UNHCR had informed them of our visit to their office. One of the officials drove us to the UNHCR house we once occupied before the great move. Well, we were happy to be back "home" at last. Although we had no idea what would happen next, we decided to enjoy the moment. We relaxed, bathed, had a good hot meal, and rested.

As I was enjoying this comfort, I remember fighting fears about the uncertainty of my future and that of the baby I was carrying. I remember looking back on the adventurous journeys I had taken within the six months, beginning from the time I left Pretoria with Joel and Monica.

As I quietly marveled at how I made it to Maputo from Casa da Morte in my pregnancy state, it dawned on me that I could not have done it with my own strength. I had just been on one of my journeys under **His Wings.**

CHAPTER 11
FROM CASA DE MORTE TO PRISON

Transitioning To The Dungeon

We arrived in Maputo on a Thursday and spent the weekend at the UNHCR house. Home at last! We began to share our felt hopes that we would be allowed to occupy the house until we were ready to leave the country. In my private thoughts, I entertained the false surety that my pregnancy would qualify me to stay in the house, regardless of what was to come next.

The exhaustion of walking for four days, and a venture which was fueled by high levels of adrenaline, was now felt by all three of us as we settled in.

I recall feeling drained as if my immune system was depleted; I was completely run down. Musa reminded me with his kind, soft voice that I could not afford to fall ill. He quickly got a syringe that he had in his emergency kit and injected me with penicillin. Musa was a nurse in South Africa.

Come to think of it; he probably got himself a few of those ampules before he left the country. I believe that the drug had probably expired already. Moreover, it was not kept in any refrigerator for preservation.

Nevertheless, this was the best medical intervention we had access to, and it worked. I rested and felt better.

After a good breakfast, Monday morning following our arrival at the house, we were taken back to the Frelimo party Head Quarters to meet with the senior officers. We expected to have a meeting where we would be given an opportunity to state our case and perhaps solicit sympathetic ears for our cause.

On our arrival at the office, I saw Monica's boyfriend, but he couldn't say much or do anything to protect me from what was coming. We were asked a few questions, which sounded like just a formality. We were then transported to a prison.

On arrival in the prison, I was relieved to find Miriam. Ahayah answered our prayer and gave us the desires of our hearts. I was hilariously excited, beside myself, happy and all those things. We were both talking to each other at the same time, allowing very little time to listen to each other's stories.

Miriam wanted to know where her husband Musa was and how he was doing. She was very pleased to know that he was on the male side of the prison along with John. It seemed like The Most High had it all arranged that we end up in prison, the only way we would know that he had answered our prayer. Yes!

We sought the Lord, and He heard us and delivered us from all our fears. .... O taste and see that the Lord is good; blessed is the man that trusteth in him. (Psalm 34: 4 and 8).

As we finally settled down, it suddenly hit me that I was IN PRISON. How can this be when I had narrowly escaped being prisoned in my country and was determined to go and fight for freedom? FREEDOM! I obviously did not have the revelation of the word FREEDOM.

Could it be that I was working hard, looking for something I could not achieve with my work and my human efforts? It felt like I was chasing the wind. 'Surely, Mozambican prisons are not likely to be as vicious as South African prisons,' I reasoned as I consoled myself.

Well, as we sat down with Miriam, she began to tell her own journey to prison. Apparently, the Frelimo Intelligence had found out that Miriam had a relative who lived in North America. She and her husband Musa had asked the UNHCR to help them to obtain refugee status in the country where they already had relatives.

At the time, apparently, North America, particularly the United States of America, was known to be an ally of the forces that were opposing Frelimo and the newly gained independence. Miriam had been taken to the Frelimo Headquarters, where she was questioned if she had anything to do with the CIA, the American Intelligence.

Following the questioning, Miriam was brought to this prison. She talked about how she continuously prayed to The Lord, asking Him to reunite her with her husband unharmed. Indeed, The Most High had now answered her prayer by bringing Musa along with John and me to the same prison.

CHAPTER 12
Prison, A Glorified Casa De Morte

Mozambican prisons were at the time overflowing with prisoners. I got to understand from other inmates that people who went into these prisons were never sure when they would be released as they were held without being sentenced. In fact, there were inmates who had been in this prison for several years already, going back to the time when the Portuguese regime was in power.

This information was very unsettling because, to me, it implied that we could be in this prison endlessly and probably die there. There were children who were born in this prison by their mothers who had been arrested while they were pregnant.

Therefore, being pregnant did not guarantee my release or put me in an advantageous stance over any of these women inmates. In fact, it seemed to me that majority of these women and their children were settled and accepted the prison as their home. Some of the women who got arrested after Frelimo had taken over told me that they had been accused of prostitution because they were seen wearing short dresses while they had gone to town for shopping.

We were kept in dormitory-style cells that had bunk beds. Life in this prison had no purpose, just as it was in Casa De Morte. The only difference was that we had clean tap water to drink and wash our bodies. We had freshly baked large-size buns with our tea for breakfast. I always looked forward to breakfast time for two reasons; buns were my favorite food, and there was also a large time gap between breakfast and our second meal, which took care of lunch and supper.

We were indeed breaking a fast by the time we had those delicious buns. Our second meal of the day consisted of macaroni mixed in a stew made from pieces of pork, beef, and sometimes some chicken pieces, all in one pot. Sometimes I could not figure out what I had just swallowed, whether it was meat, what kind of meat, or something else. Hey! If you didn't like greasy food, you would starve because that was our everyday menu.

Having lived in Casa De Morte, the prison was indeed a glorified version of our camp experience. At least we were in Maputo, not in the bush. That gave us hope that one day we would be free.

Every morning we were to form a line and match like soldiers to the gate of the prison where we were trained to shout certain slogans, such as: "Viva (live long) Samora Machel, viva Frelimo, Abaixa prostituicao (Down with prostitution)! Abaixa capitalismo (down with capitalism) ! We were told that there was no God. I am not sure what would have happened to anyone who would dare to explicitly practice some kind of religion outside the indoctrination that was being instilled in all inmates. In fact, a good number of the inmates who were arrested during the Frelimo regime at the time belonged to the Jehovah's Witness sect.

All this kind of indoctrination went on day in and day out. Deep down in my spirit, there was a war going on that began to intensify before the morning drill and for about three to four hours after the drill. I had been raised in a Christian home, my father being a minister of the gospel.

I knew no other truth but that there is only one God, The Most High, Ahayah, along with His begotten Son, Christ, and the Holy Spirit. I surely understand why David was infuriated and disgusted when Goliath, the Philistine most daring giant man of the time, went out to defy the armies of the living God of Israel. David said:

....for who is this uncircumcised Philistine that he should defy the armies of the living God" (1 Samuel 17:26; KJV).

David had been raised to not only know about The Most High, Ahayah, but he himself also had first-hand experience with the God of his fathers. He believed in Him wholeheartedly. He knew that The Most High, the God of Israel, was not just a figure of a man's imagination that could be easily substituted by theories and opinions of mankind. David had experienced his God in action when He protected and rescued him from the lions and bares. David said:

The Lord that delivered me out of the paw of the lion and out of the paw of the bear He will deliver me out of the hand of this Philistine. (1Samuel 17:37, KJV).

David was able to fight a physical war and won. The Most High had used him to defeat the blasphemous man and his army through this adolescent boy who would dare to believe Him.

Fighting the spiritual Goliath

During my internal spiritual struggle, I began to remember how this God, whom my parents had taught me to know and receive as my Protector quite early in life, had made Himself known to me countless times. I had journeyed many times under His Wings. As a matter of fact, I had just completed a journey from Casa De Morte to this prison with my two friends, John and Musa, under His Wings. How about the miraculous journey I had along with Joel and Monica, from South Africa to Mozambique?

When challenges of life seem to be overwhelming, taking stock of The Most High's promises and how He has been faithful in your life can become a solid bridge through which you can cross those troubled waters. Often times when life seems to go well, the tendency for most of us is to forget that all good things, including the blessings that bring wealth and prosperity, come from The Most High God.

Moses had a revelation about mankind's weakness when the Holy Spirit urged him to warn Israel not to forget The Most High; how He had delivered them from Egypt. And from the armies of Pharaoh. (Deuteronomy 8: 13- 17).

When I began to realize the seriousness of my captivity, having no hope of ever being released, I had to resort to going back to what was familiar to me, trusting The Most High. I made up my mind that I would not repeat the slogans during the morning assembly at the gate. Since I was not bold enough to openly defy the prison wardens, I began to make excuses that would be valid enough for me to stay in my cell and miss the morning drill at the gate. Sometimes I would hide behind other inmates and avoid being noticed by the wardens that I was only moving my lips and not repeating the slogans as was required.

The Angel's Visitation

One day in July 1976, a few hours after our second and last meal of the day, I experienced stomach cramps and was running a fever. I went to bed earlier than usual, hoping that rest would resolve my physical discomfort. I had an amazing but frightening vision that left a remarkable impression in my mind for many years.

I saw in my dream a Shemitic looking Bantu/Black old man with a grey beard who came and sat before me. I recall wondering if this person could be my paternal grandfather due to some familiarity with his appearance. By the way, I had never seen my grandfather in real life, as he died before I was born, nor did I ever see his picture. Although this old-looking man was kind and spoke like a caring father, I could not look at his face and converse with him. I immediately bowed down with reverence, fear, and awe. He said these words: "My child, ask me for anything, and I will give it to you."

Words could not come out of my mouth; I did not know what and how to tell him the long list of my desires. I responded only with my thoughts. I began to think about the child I was carrying, the captivity I was in with no hope for release, and whether I would ever be free. It felt like the vision lasted for about half an hour; I then woke up still feeling quite shaken.

I stayed in bed pondering about this vision. I remember feeling a sense of frustration and disappointment with myself for not speaking out about what I had in mind. Surely, I was desperate to leave the prison; the thought of having a baby in jail was haunting me daily. The stomach pains and flu-like feeling I was still experiencing had intensified these fears.

Faith and Hope Re-Kindled

As the early rises of the sun were beginning to penetrate through the tiny windows of my prison cell, I stepped out of my bunk bed while all the other inmates were still asleep. I took my metal mug, went to the toilet, and got some water from a small tap. I began to do what I saw my father used to do; I prayed, reciting the Lord's Prayer over the water with deep conviction, and drank it.

It was a confession prayer, repenting for my sins, and it was a prayer for my healing which I desperately needed. After this private prayer time, I went back to my bed and lay down. The pains suddenly stopped, the fever lifted, and I regained my strength. The Most High heard my prayer and responded according to His word in Psalm 34;

I sought the Lord, and He heard me, and delivered me from all my fears.......This poor man cried, and the Lord heard him and saved him out of all his troubles. (Psalm 34: 4; 6. KJV)

Yes! Clearly, my faith had been re-kindled by the vision I had in my dream. Obviously, my healing had little or nothing to do with the water; I believe it was faith to which The Most High responded. In retrospection, I believe that The Most High had sent one of His angels to bring solutions to my dilemmas. It seemed it didn't really matter that I could not respond in the dream. This experience began to fuel hope and assurance that there was going to be an end to my captivity.

The President's Visit

A few days after this supernatural experience, I was standing outside the cell when the President of Mozambique, Samora Machel, walked through the prison gates. He saw me standing and walked towards me; I was quite conspicuous at this point since I was already within my 8th month of pregnancy.

He said these words in si-Zulu, one of the South African Bantu dialects, "Why are you here? What brought you here?" I ran out of words and did not know where to begin giving him my story, although I felt this would be the opportunity to finally have a sympathetic listener. I experienced mixed emotions; I was shocked to see the President, excited, and felt privileged; I simply answered, "I don't know."

I quickly told him that I was not the only one who had been arrested. I informed him that I had another sister here and two other South African men. He left me and moved on to inspect the prison, which was overflowing with women and a few children.

Three weeks later, I, with my three comrades, were released to the UN house from where we were removed. We were subsequently flown to Tanzania, where we were received and accommodated by the African National Congress, one of the South African liberation movements at the time.

Approximately two weeks after our arrival in Tanzania, I gave birth to a healthy baby, my daughter. The Most High had protected the child in-utero throughout the experiences we had in Mozambique.

It is important to inform the reader of this testimony that Mozambique was still trying to regroup while rebuilding the nation after Frelimo had overthrown the Portuguese colonial regime. Running to Mozambique shortly after they had obtained their independence was obviously not a wise move on our part. However, we were young and naïve to think that we were going to have our dreams fulfilled while the country was still a war zone.

Yes, although Frelimo had won the victory against the Portuguese army, we later learned that there were still black soldiers who had sided with the Portuguese army and who continued to engage in a guerrilla war against the Frelimo.

CHAPTER 13
PERSUIT OF FREEDOM THROUGH EDUCATION

After settling for a few months in Tanzania, my dream to further my studies was re-kindled. Although living among other South African freedom fighters was comforting, my vision of how to attain this freedom was different from those who were around me. I believed that it was important for me to attain the highest level of university education. I reasoned that with high education I could earn respect from other races, particularly the Caucasian. I would also gain a status high enough to attain freedom and escape racism.

I remember being informed that I would be sent to the then Soviet Union for military training as soon as the baby was old enough to be left in the care of older women within the ANC. Well, I quietly visited a UNHCR office in Dar Es Salaam, which was at the time the capital city of Tanzania. I applied for scholarship which would enable me to pursue university education. UNHCR got me admitted at the University of Ibadan in Nigeria where I enrolled for a three-year BSc Honors degree in Psychology.

Divine Plan to Scale Off Psychological Scars of Racism

It was comforting to live among other black people where I did not feel degraded or made to feel like less important than an animal. However, I continued to feel restless, discontent, and experienced void within my spirit. I marveled as I observed people of my race who freely married white people and not get arrested or brutally ostracized. I experienced discomfort and cognitive dissonance in that on one hand I was acknowledging a level of freedom, yet on the other hand I thought it was too good to be true. The question is, was I free? Perhaps, internally the scars of racism were still bleeding. I was too resentful and full of hatred towards anyone who looked like my South African oppressors. I was NOT free.

During the first year of my degree, one of my lecturers was a white Jewish woman, Naomi, who was born and grew up in South Africa. She, her husband and their three children were in Nigeria, her husband an engineer on a contract. They had left South Africa in the late 60s to live in Scotland. She began to take interest in me when she learned that I was also a South African. She perceived that I was uncomfortable around her and avoided any interactions with her outside the lecture room.

One day Naomi informed me that she was against the discriminating racial laws of the Apartheid South African government, and that she also had to leave the country for that reason. Subsequently, Naomi invited me for an afternoon meal at her home. I did not believe her "comforting" confession, nevertheless, I reluctantly accepted the invitation.

I arrived at her house while she was busy preparing the meal. I was warmly welcome and made to feel comfortable after being offered a glass of juice. As soon as she had finished preparing food, before we ate, she quickly went to have a shower in her room. After a while I had Naomi calling me to come to her room. I thought she needed the help of her maiden (me, a slave). I reluctantly went to her not knowing what to expect. I found her drying her naked body with a towel while she casually chatted with me. I nearly collapsed but held myself together.

This behavior may appear grossly inappropriate, and it felt that way to me as well. However, the reader may not know that the body of a white woman was sacred in South Africa. A-Bantu were severely punished, beaten up and or killed if by accident they saw a naked white woman. I was completely petrified and almost shaking not knowing what to do as the thoughts of what could happen to me. She smiled and said she wanted me to see that she was an ordinary woman like me with the same body anatomy. The Most High used her to help scale off some of the psychological scars I had which had fueled resentment and hatred for the Caucasian race.

The Most High's Hand In Fulfilling My Human Efforts To Attain Freedom Through Education.

The Lord will perfect that which concerneth me: thy mercy, O Lord, endureth for ever: forsake not the works of thine own hands. (Psalm 138: 8. KJV)

In Nigeria it was comforting to meet other South African refugees who were studying at various universities, including medical school. However, I experienced a level of culture shock and felt unsettled. At the beginning of my second university year, I began to explore possibility of transferring to The United States of America, a land of 'opportunities'. I got excited to receive positive response from several universities.

While I was thinking of approaching the UNHCR for transferring my scholarship to America, The Most High gave me a vision in my dream. In this dream I knelt in front of an old Bantu looking man who seemed to possess a high level of authority. His seat was in front of what looked like a stage with heavy closed drapes behind him. I knelt with my face down with fear and reverence. I also felt the presence of angels behind me, on my left and right sides. Behind the drapes I heard a voice of a man which sounded like that of my father praying in a language I could not recognized. It felt like he was praying, interceding for me for about 30 minutes and stopped.

It is important to share that in 1978 when I had just arrived in Nigeria, I received a telegram that my father had died. It was already a month after he was buried that I got to know about his passing on to be with his forefathers. Therefore, hearing a praying voice in this vision, which sounded like my father was comforting, to say the least.

However, I believe that the praying voice was that of Yashaya Christ, our High Priest (Hebrews 4:15) and the mediator between The Most High God and men (1 Timothy: 2) but not my father, since he was already resting in Abraham's bosom.

When the praying voice stopped, I heard one of the beings behind me saying "Please give it to her". The Man of authority in front of me responded, "but she does NOT pray". The angel said, "but she does sometimes pray The Lord's Prayer". I woke up from the dream shaking in fear.

Following this encounter, I again got another dream a week or two later. This time I heard a voice but could not see the person talking. It was speaking with intense authority saying, "I am NOT sending you to America but to Canada". I again woke up, but this time feeling puzzled.

I was puzzled because I could not imagine how I could possibly get to Canada. The reason was that some of our South African refugees studying in Nigeria had made attempts to get to Canada but without success. They told me that from their experience, Canadian embassy was refusing South African refugees, student visas or to grant them refugee status.

Nevertheless, I began to apply to few Canadian universities and got accepted. However, I did not know how to proceed any further, and decided to complete my three-year BSc. Honors at the University of Ibadan and waited for The Most High's promise to be fulfilled.

Execution of The Most High's Plan through a Miraculous Envelope.

God is not a man, that he should lie; neither the son of man, that he should repent: hath he said, and shall he not do it? Or hath he spoken, and shall he not make it good? (Numbers 23: 19. KJV)

In 1982, after I had completed my studies in Nigeria, I moved to Lesotho, a small country located inside South Africa. Although it is surrounded by South Africa, Lesotho was and is a sovereign country which is ruled by Bantu leaders. One of the benefits of living in Lesotho was that my family could visit me, including my daughters who I had not seen for several years.

In addition, one of my brothers who had survived torture and imprisonment in South Africa had escaped to Lesotho with his family. Living in this country provided a relatively safe home for South African refugees, including freedom fighters under the ANC leadership. However, it was also not completely safe in that it served as back-yard for South African Apartheid soldiers who often went in and out of Lesotho, disguised as ordinary civilians or tourist.

In Lesotho I got employed by the government as a counsellor, with my BSc. Honors degree in Psychology, working in a psychiatric hospital. I lived in Maseru city and was accommodated in one of the government houses. In July 1982, I received an envelope delivered to my place of residence with my full name written on it. I found it at my doorstep when I returned from work. Those years it was common for the Apartheid regime to secretly send bombs to South African

following the December 1982 Maseru massacre during which my mother, my children, my brother, and his family narrowly escaped death. The South African soldiers had invaded Maseru city in Lesotho and targeted all areas where refugees from South Africa lived. They also raided the homes where I used to live and killed many people. Surely if I was still in Maseru I would have been killed since the massacre was carried by night.

My Life in Winnipeg, Manitoba. Canada

As I settled in Canada, I began to relax and was becoming comfortable living among different races without always being on guard. I worked hard and completed my Master's degree in 1986. I continued with my studies and attained the "highest level of my education" the Doctorate degree I had set out to accomplish to gain "freedom". My mother visited me and attended my graduation ceremonies for both degrees.

Well! The question remained, did I get my real freedom, at least from The Most High's perspective? From the human point of view, since He facilitated my path to fulfilment of my dreams, it made sense to believe that my "high level" of education was what I needed to attain freedom from racism. I hole-heartedly believed that it would cushion me from being segregated and being treated less than an animal because of my race.

Why don't you go to church?

Despite my accomplishment, I continued to feel a void within me as if something was still missing. I tried to fill up this void by keeping myself busy, taking on side jobs while I was still a full-time Doctorate student and a full-time parent.

One Saturday night I had a vision in my dream. I heard a voice sounding like the one I heard praying in my dream while I was in Nigeria. This time this male voice spoke with intense reprimanding tone, asking me <u>"why don't you go to church?"</u>. At the time I was not attending any church although I regarded myself as belonging to Anglican Christian denomination. I was so shaken by this reprimanding vision that I got up on Sunday morning and went to attend an Anglican church service. The service had already begun, and the congregation was singing a hymn. I put my handbag down on the floor while standing and joined in with the singing. As soon as we set down at the end of the hymn, I heard a loud voice saying "what are you doing here? Go to church". I looked around to check if anyone else heard this voice. I quickly stood up, grabbed my handbag, and left the building terrified. One might think I was hallucinating (a psychological term for someone who is hearing voices when no one else hears them).

It is important to share that on a previous Friday, a day before my visit to this church, while I was at work, one of the secretaries, Dorothy, approached me and asked to have coffee time with her. I honored this invitation cheerfully. During our visit she asked me if I knew anything about Christ. I chuckled and responded, "of cause I do". I proceeded to tell her that my father was a minister of the gospel and that I grew up in a Christian home. She then asked me if I really had a relationship with Christ. To this end, I boastfully informed her that The Most High often spoke to me through dreams and that I was quite fine. She told me that there was a more and richer experience to having a prayer life and getting to have a close relationship with Christ. She proceeded to invite me to a church service which was to be held on Saturday, the following day. She informed me that a visiting evangelist was going to be at this service. I accepted this invitation and attended the service. While the evangelist was preaching, I had interesting but frightening experience. I found myself confessing to Dorothy everything I have ever done wrong in my whole life. After this confession I felt a weight lifted from inside me. She then invited me to go to her church for the next day Sunday service. I did not promise but said I would think about it. Well, I went home and forgot about her.

The next day, after having the reprimanding dream and subsequently hearing the voice while I was at the Anglican church, I went straight to Dorothy's church and joined her for the service. As I sat next to her and her husband, she informed me that she was praying for me to show up for the service. At this church service, I felt a change within me and asked to be water baptized with the rest of the people who were getting baptized that day.

Was The Most High God, Ahayah redirecting me to more meaningful freedom? Well, the scripture tells us that His thoughts are NOT our thoughts, neither are our ways His ways (Isaiah 55:8). Clearly, what I considered as the path to freedom was not how The Most High wanted me to attain it, but through His Son Yashaya Christ. After all He made it clear in Isaiah 55 verse 9 that:

For as the heavens are higher than the earth, so are my ways higher than your ways, and my thoughts than your thoughts (KJV).

Home Coming Family Reunion

In 1992, I visited South Africa for the first time since 1975 when I fled to exile. I was warmly welcome by my immediate and extended family members. It was a very emotional experience to return to my parents' home and be reminded that my father had passed on. Although I was informed almost two decades before then, being home without seeing him made me realize that I needed a closure. My mother and my siblings organized a celebration, highlighting my education success.

Yes, I was successful in my own right, and perhaps accomplished what I had purposed to attain, freedom through education. However, I came back with a better understanding that freedom could not be attained through education alone without having a meaningful relationship with The Most High God through His Son Yashaya Christ. It was important for me to share with my family the spiritual experience which reshaped my life. An experience which perhaps I would not have had without journeying under His Wings.

CHAPTER 14
MY ORIGIN, MY TRUE IDENTITY

And you shall know the truth, and The Truth shall make you free

(John 8:32; KJV)

In the previous chapters, I shared how my friends and I managed to escape the brutal harassment and arrest by the police of the Apartheid government, which led us to a sudden unplanned journey of no return to our homeland. The purpose of this journey naturally progressed from running for safety to a quest for "freedom." This quest, in my mind, could be attained outside the borders of South Africa where, as I believed, I would gain respect and be appreciated as a Black or Bantu-Ngoni or Negro or African (or all of these).

Yes, "Black" because of my brown skin pigmentation; Umtu (singular of A-Bantu); South African, as a native of the country where I was born. It is in this very country where I was also referred to by the ruling masters as "Kaffir", a by-word with a negative connotation equivalent to "Nigger" word. Nigger is a word often used in America to refer to people of my race who are recognized as "Negroes". As I researched, I found the meaning of the word Kaffir as follows:

Kaffir *is a racist slur used to refer to an individual of Abantu ancestry. In the form of cafri, it evolved during the pre-colonial period as an equivalent of "negro". (Wikipedia definition)*

The Dictionary.com defines the word Kaffir as follows:

noun, plural **Kaf·firs,** *(especially collectively)* **Kaf·fir.**

Extremely Disparaging and Offensive. (in South Africa) a contemptuous term used to refer to a Black person: originally used of the Xhosa people only.

Notwithstanding, I must share how I felt quite despondent and sad after listening to the Christian leaders I referred to earlier on in the previous chapter, who identified me as a Hamite. I felt trapped when I realized that there was no hope for an end to the suffering of this Negro/A-Bantu race, due to our "Hamitic bloodline." It was at this point that I decided to do some independent research on the Hamitic lineage to have a better-informed understanding of who these people are.

The first natural thing for me to do was to search the dictionary for a definition of the word Hamitic, Hamite, or Ham. The Zondervan Bible Dictionary gives me the following:

Ham (him, perhaps hot). The youngest son of Noah, born probably about 96 years before the Flood, and one of eight persons to live through the Flood. He became the progenitor of the dark races, not the Negroes (my emphasis), but the Egyptians, Ethiopians, Libyans, and Canaanites (Gen. 10: 6-20). (Zondervan Bible Dictionary). His indecency, when his father lay drunken, brought a curse upon Canaan (Gen. 9: 20-27). ..Ham is used as another name for Egypt as representing Ham's principal descendants. (Pages 213-214).

Well! This was an eye opener, which led me to also read what Zondervan Bible Dictionary (page 401) writes about Nimrod, since the "curse" from which I am supposed to be suffering, as identified by these Christian leaders, originates from being "his descendent." This is what I found:

Nimrod, son of Cush; hunter, Nineveh and kingdoms in Shinar (Gen 10: 8-12).

On Cush, Zondervan Bible Dictionary (Page 120) writes:

Cush (Kush), the oldest son of Ham, one of the three sons of Noah (Gen. 10:6-8)

Clearly, according to these findings, the Negro/Bantu race is not included in the lineage of Ham and/or Nimrod. The next logical thing I could do was to check out The Bible since The Creator of mankind, and all creation is also The Author of The Bible. I studied the lineage of the other two sons of Noah, Shem, and Japheth.

Through my research, I also learned that my Black race did not descend from Japheth either. I realized that Shem was the grandfather of Abraham, the father of Isaac, and the grandfather of Jacob, who was later named Israel. Through my further biblical study, it became clear that the Blacks are the descendants of Israel and are Shemites or Semites.

Why Jacob or Israel as the forefather of the Negroes and not his twin brother Esau or Edom?

The reader may be interested to know. This is a logical question; however, attempting to answer or elaborate on the subject will be outside the scope of this book. The reader is encouraged to read the Bible and other supplementary books referenced in the Bible about the twin brothers Jacob and Esau; what The Most High told Rebecca, their mother, concerning the unborn twins; how they looked like at birth; and the account on the rest of their lives. In fact, the Zondervan Bible Dictionary (page 141) says about Edom:

Edom, Edomites (e dom, Edomites, red), the nation and its people who were the descendants of Esau. He founded the country, so his name is equated with Edom (Genesis 25:30; 36: 1, 8). The country was also called Seir, or Mt. Seir, which was the name of the territory in which the Edomites lived.

Why, then, are the so-called Blacks referred to as Negroes (Niger-Black)?

In searching the meaning of the word Negro and its origin, I got to understand that the term was first used in the New Testament, where the disciples of Yashaya, The Messiah Christ, were first described as Negroes in Antioch.

Now there were in the church that was at Antioch certain prophets and teachers; as Barnabas, and Simeon that was called Niger, ...(Acts 13: 1; KJV)

I got excited when I realized from this scripture verse that the disciples of The Messiah were identified as Negroes. It made sense then that Paul was once mistaken as one of the original Hamitic Egyptians, who were also dark-skinned.

Art not thou that Egyptian, which before these days madest an uproar, and leddest out into the wilderness four thousand men that were murderers? (Acts 21: 38, KJV).

However, in Romans 11 verse 1, Paul made it clear that he was "an Israelite, of the seed of Abraham, of the tribe of Benjamin."

Likewise, when they arrived in Egypt and saw their brother Joseph, the sons of Jacob were convinced that he was an Egyptian (Genesis 42 to 45) until he revealed himself. We also read that Moses, a Levite, was mistaken to be an Egyptian by the seven daughters of the Midian priest when he fled to the land of Midian (Exodus 2: 19).

At this point, I began to wonder if Yashaya, the Messiah Himself, was a Negro! Mhh! Since his disciples were identified as Negroes (Acts 13:1). Well, I remember that The Most High did instruct Yashaya's biological father, Joseph, to flee to Egypt with the baby and his mother, Mary, to hide there when Herod was planning to kill him. (Matthew 2:13).

What a perfect place to hide among other dark-skinned people where he and his parents could blend in with the Egyptians. Furthermore, as I searched the scriptures, I found out that John, the revelator in chapter one of the book of Revelation, described the features of Christ as he saw Him in his vision as follows:

And I turned to see the voice that spake with me. And being turned, I saw seven golden candlesticks; And in the midst of the seven candlesticks one like unto the Son of man, clothed with a garment down to the foot, and girt about the paps with a golden girdle. **His head and his hairs were white like wool**, *as white as snow, and his eyes were as a flame of fire.* **And his feet like unto fine brass, as if they burned in a furnace;** *and his voice as the sound of many waters. (Rev. 1:12-15. KJV)*

Well, according to this scripture reference, Yashaya's hair, as seen by John, was wooly, the same texture as that of the Negroes. Also, the color of His feet (which must look like His whole body) looked like brass burned in a furnace (dark brown or black, like Negroes complexion).

CHAPTER 15
Desperate Prayer in Search of The Truth

In my distress, I found myself speaking out loud a short prayer to The Most High, asking Him to reveal to me the true doctrine of Christ, the Messiah whose physical appearance looked like mine.

I needed to know and understand the gospel, which was preached by the original disciples of Yashaya, The Messiah, people like Peter, John, Paul, and other early followers of Christ. At this moment, I was desperate to know what the early church or original Christians knew about people of my race since these disciples were also identified as Negroes.

Shortly after this prayer, I received a revelation concerning the existence of the twelve tribes of Israel. When The Most High revealed this understanding, many questions flocked to my mind. I began to wonder who and where these tribes were; how come I had never heard any preacher talking about them and identifying their whereabouts on earth today?

I again asked my Christian leaders if they knew about these tribes and if they could identify them. I was informed that they were scattered all over the earth; they were lost and could not be identified. The irony, though, is that these leaders also believed that the Caucasians who today reside in the land of Israel and are identified as Jewish people are regarded as 'the' chosen people of God. Hmm! I thought, why did The Most High inform me about the twelve tribes of Israel; surely there was a significant reason.

An urgent desire to learn more about these tribes and their biblical history began to grow stronger. Nevertheless, my quest for ultimate freedom for me as a Black person and that of my race was still the focus. I could not understand why we were often disrespected, oppressed, and enslaved by other races on earth; why we tend to be easy targets for incurable diseases, killer vaccine Guinea pigs, including generational poverty, irrespective of where we live in this world.

What, then, is the Justification For the Oppression of The Negroes/Bantus?

While I was pondering on this matter, The Most High led me to a YouTube broadcast and listened to one of the teachings taught by the Elders of The Gathering of Christ Church, who talked about these twelve tribes. These teachers addressed the issues concerning the suffering often experienced by these scattered tribes as fulfilling the curses described in the book of

Deuteronomy chapter 28 in the Bible. I began to study it with much zeal and intensity.

I must admit that Deuteronomy 28 is one of my favorite Books in the Bible as a Christian, on which I used to focus but only on verses 1 to 13. Yes, these are some of the verses which strengthened my beliefs in God, whose purpose in mind was to only bless me.

You see! I was taught by my Christian preachers that if I accepted Jesus as my Lord and Savior, I would be grafted into the nation of Israel. This meant that by faith, I could now be the descendant of Abraham and partake of all these blessings written in Deuteronomy 28:1-13. In fact, I enjoyed quoting verse 13 the most, which reads:

The Lord shall make thee the head and not the tail; thou shall be above only, and thou shall not be beneath;

As a Christian and a Bantu, it was comforting to me to believe that by praying this verse and claiming my "rights" as an adopted child of Abraham through Christ, I could rise above my oppressors and gain the freedom for which I was longing. However, I would never complete this verse 13, nor did I feel the need to understand its entire message. I often ignored the rest of the verse, which reads:

If that thou hearken unto the commandments of the Lord thy God, which I command thee this day, to observe and to do them.

I must admit that quoting and praying the first part of this verse did not solve my dilemma; I was still black and a Bantu, belonging to a race that continues to be beneath and not above only. Obviously, the fulfillment of the promise in the first part of the verse is contingent on carrying out the instructions stated in the second part of the verse.

It demands that I observe and keep the commandments of The Most High God which were given to the children of Israel through Moses.

At this point, I had to either believe the scriptures as The Word of The Most High or reject it and believe what my Christian teachers, who told me that I didn't need to observe these laws and commandments because they were done away with. I was taught that Yashaya (which means My Savior), whom the world refers to as Jesus, had fulfilled all the laws and commandments of the Old Testament.

As such, this part of the verse was not relevant to my walk as a Christian. This understanding protected me from experiencing cognitive dissonance, although the promise stated in the first part of Deuteronomy 28 verse 13 is now obviously contingent on the fulfillment of the second part. I was completely spiritually blinded to this understanding and lacked wisdom.

What often puzzled me, though, was that I was still struggling in life like all the people of my race, although in my Sunday worship Christianity, I had supposedly fulfilled all requirements to enjoy the blessings listed in Deuteronomy 28. What, then, was the missing piece of this puzzle which could provide me with a way out of this dilemma?

Well, as I continued to listen to the information taught by these Christian teachers of the Bible, I began to study the entire chapter of Deuteronomy 28, using the King James version of the Bible. To my great surprise, I realized that there was a group of people to whom Moses, a descendant of Israel, was instructing to keep and do The Most High's laws and commandments.

Since the release of these blessings was contingent on total obedience to these laws, this group of people would not escape the curses stated in verses 15 to 68. What shocked me was my observation that every one of these curses mirrored the very experiences I and the people of my race who are in Southern Africa, the African continent, and all over the world suffer.

I became very curious to know who these people were. I realized that these were the descendants of the twelve tribes of Israel.

These people were instructed to diligently observe, keep, and do the laws, statutes, and commandments of The God of Israel perpetually throughout all generations unto the end. Moses made it clear that failing to do so would cause all children of Israel to suffer the curses listed in Deuteronomy 28:15-68.

In the previous chapter, I established through my research that the so-called Black people or Negroes or Bantu-Ngoni are the descendants of Shem, one of the three sons of Noah, and not of Ham. Therefore, we are of Shematic lineage through Abraham, Isaac, and Jacob or Israel, the Shemite of the Semite family.

Thus, our suffering as a nation and race has nothing to do with curses related to Ham, Canaan, and/or Nimrod whatsoever since we belong to a Shematic lineage.

However, as The Most High God continued to open my understanding, I still questioned the reasons for the miserable conditions under which my people and I in South Africa are subjected. I became motivated to study Deuteronomy chapter 28 to find answers.

In observing all nations of the world and their races, I could not find anyone who had ever experienced all these curses listed in this chapter in biblical proportion, except for the Negro race as well as the so-called indigenous peoples of the world, like the aboriginals in Australia, New Zealand; so-called American Indians, Hispanics, etc.; as well as the indigenous people of Southern Africa, who are referred to as Khoi-San. The highlight of these curses is in verse 68, which reads:

And the Lord shall bring thee into Egypt again with ships, by the way whereof I spake unto thee, Thou shall see it no more again: and there ye shall be sold unto your enemies for bondmen and bondwomen, and no man shall buy you. (Deut. 28:68. KJV)

Well! I know no other group of people who had been shipped as slaves in large numbers and who are still being carried away as slaves in ships today other than negroes or so-called Africans.

I went back to The Most High and asked who these people were and where can we find them. Are the Negroes/Abantu included in these twelve tribes?

He gave me a positive response which led me to ask more questions: "which tribe am I part of?" He confirmed that I am a descendant of the tribe of Judah. Well! When I got this answer, I made sure that I got confirmation since the scripture instructs us to test every spirit.

I must confess that when I got this confirmation, I felt mixed emotions. I did not know whether to cry or to laugh, with the joy of knowing that I finally knew my true identity. Cry because, throughout my life, I knew myself as a Xhosa woman and a Bantu; yet in reading the Bible, I could not find Xhosa people. Joy, because now I knew that my journey, which all along had been under His Wings for obtaining meaningful freedom, was just beginning.

CHAPTER 16
KNOWING ONE'S IDENTITY: A KEY TO FREEDOM

The question is, did our people attain true "freedom"? What is really missing in this picture? Why is it that among the people who live in the country of South Africa today, the Caucasians, East Indians, and recently, Chinese, our people, the negro race remains being visibly and negatively affected by this trodden horse, the "Freedom" or "Independence"? Independence from what? What, then, is the real Freedom for the Negroes? How can it be obtained? Could it be that all along, we have been looking for freedom in the wrong places and using the wrong methods to find it?

PATH TO TRUE FREEDOM FOR JACOB'S DESCENDANTS

In the previous chapters, I established beyond doubt that most of these people who are identified as Africans, Blacks, or

Negroes are the descendants of Jacob or Israel. They are Shemites or Semites, the descendants of Shem, one of the sons of Noah. What relevance does this fact have in our people gaining freedom? After all, we tried everything we had in our power to attain freedom.

From Ahayah's perspective, as found in the Scriptures, Israel can attain real freedom by accepting His plans of redemption for His people through Yashaya Christ, who would free us from the bondage of sin and death to righteousness and everlasting life. Yashaya spoke these words of wisdom to the Israelites who believed in Him:

If ye continue in my word, then are ye my disciples indeed; And ye shall know the truth, and the truth shall make you free (John 8: 31-32 KJV).

Note that Yashaya here was talking to people of his race/nation, the Israelites, who were also His followers. However, it seems, despite them knowing their identity as Israelites, they still needed to continue in His word and know the truth as **their path to freedom.**

When I finally understood this fact, I had this strong desire to find the path which would lead me to freedom. After all, it is evident that our plan to bring freedom to our people through military training, nationwide protests, and organized liberation movements had dismally failed. Paul warned that:

For though we walk in the flesh, we do not war after the flesh; For the weapons of our warfare are not carnal, but mighty through God to the pulling down imaginations, and every high thing that exalteth itself against the knowledge of God and bringing into captivity every thought to the obedience of Christ (II Corinthians 10:3-5. KJV).

Nevertheless, this truth was far from being realized in my life at the time. I needed a schoolmaster, real-life experience. Indeed! It was to take the real-life experience I was about to taste in order to understand that freedom obtained through fleshly human efforts is fake and unfulfilling.

My life experiences have opened my eyes to understanding that knowing my identity is the most important factor in gaining freedom. Indeed, knowing that I am a daughter of Judah and a descendant of Israel, as revealed to me by The Most High, has become one of my precious keys to freedom.

Up to the time when I began to grasp this truth, I was content in knowing that I was a Xhosa woman, a Bantu, Black, and an African. However, learning that as a "Hamite," I was condemned to a life under a permanent "nonredeemable" curse of Canaan was unsettling. When I realized that people had assigned this identity to me and not the Creator, I began to step on my path to freedom.

Likewise, it is an observable truth that most of our people/races all over the world do NOT know their true identity. They identify themselves, like I did, as Negroes, Bantus, Africans, and/or Blacks.

Not knowing one's genealogy places one at a disadvantage stance and vulnerability, which opens for others to give one any form of identity. It goes without saying that people who know their genealogy are readily positioned to also receive inheritance due to them.

For example, a young man who grows up raised by his father, knowing his grandfather, and great-grandfather, gets to know his identity, his lineage, as well as his family culture. He receives or expects to receive his inheritance and determines to carry on his family legacy.

He takes on and protects the family name, which in turn, he passes on to his son. This used to be a true scenario when I was growing up in South Africa in the 50s and 60s or up to the time I left for exile in the mid-70s.

On the other hand, a child who grows up in an orphanage group home may not know his identity, his real name, and his lineage. He is disjointed from the continuity of his original lineage and his family name. He is given any name and grows up believing that he is who he has been named to be.

In my book "Parenting The Remnant Generation," I discuss the importance and significance of naming a child and how this name can shape the future of a child as he or she acknowledges to be his or her true identity.

IS KNOWING ONE'S GENEALOGY AS AN ISRAELITE ENOUGH TO FIND THE PATH TO FREEDOM?

During His lifetime here on earth, Yashaya also taught His people a higher level of observing these laws and commandments, He also observed. I have learned that these laws and commandments were given to Moses on Mount Sinai by Yashaya Himself, who was then identified as The Angel of the Lord.

(For further edification, the reader is encouraged to read The Book of Jubilees 1:28; Exodus 23: 20-22; Acts 7:38-39; and 1 Corinthians 10:1-4).

Moses clearly warned the children of Israel in Deuteronomy chapter 28 that if they practiced and obeyed these laws and commandments perpetually throughout all their generations, the children of Israel would always have their freedom and be above all nations of the earth.

Since we began to follow other nations' ways of life, worshiping their gods, our God of Israel, Ahayah, began to scatter us throughout the world and had us live under all the curses stated in Deuteronomy 28:15-65. This is how we became slaves and lower than all other nations.

Notwithstanding, I later found the path to freedom as I began to understand that part of continuing in Christ's word was to keep and obey the commandments which were given ONLY to the nation of Israel. Notwithstanding, it goes without saying that knowing one's identity as an Israelite will NOT lead to real freedom if one does NOT continue in Christ's word and follow His doctrine.

Therefore, the Israelites had the responsibility to not only keep and obey these commandments but also to teach other nations to revere the God of Israel, Ahayah Ashar Ahayah, through His Son, Yashaya Christ.

Indeed, when I understood this truth, I began to pay attention to these laws and commandments, following them according to the doctrine thought by Yashaya Christ and how he Himself obeyed them, including going into **water baptism**. Therefore, I submit that this is THE PATH TO REAL FREEDOM, not only for the descendants of Jacob or Israel but for all races of the world.

We are getting closer to the return of our Savior Christ coming for His own, as He did before, and for the gentiles who worship the true God of Israel, keeping His laws, statutes, and commandments. Jacob's trouble will intensify, and only the remnant of Jacob's descendants will be saved.

Esaias also crieth concerning Israel; though the number of children of Israel is as the sand of the sea, a remnant shall be saved. (Romans 9:27).

APPENDIX

1985 PARLIAMENT SPEECH BY MR. BOTHA, PRIME MINISTER OF THE REPUBLIC OF SOUTH AFRICA

"Pretoria has been made by the White mind for the White man. We are not obliged even the least to try to prove to anybody and to the Blacks that we are superior people. We have demonstrated that to the Blacks in a thousand and one ways. The Republic of South Africa that we know today has not been created by wishful thinking. We have created it at the expense of intelligence, sweat, and blood. Were they Afrikaners who tried to eliminate the Australian Aborigines?

Are they Afrikaners who discriminate against Blacks and call them Niggers in the States? Were they Afrikaners who started the slave trade? Where is the Black man appreciated? England discriminates against its Black, and their "Sus" law is out to discipline the Blacks. Canada, France, Russia, and Japan all play their discrimination too. Why in the hell, then, is so much noise made about us? Why are they biased against us? I am simply trying to prove to you all that there is nothing unusual we are doing that the so-called civilized worlds are not doing.

We are simply honest people who have come out aloud with a clear philosophy of how we want to live our own White life.

We do not pretend like other Whites that we like Blacks. The fact that Blacks look like human beings and act like human beings does not necessarily make them sensible human beings.

Hedgehogs are not porcupines, and lizards are not crocodiles simply because they look alike.

If God wanted us to be equal to the Blacks, he would have created us all of a uniform colour and intellect. But he created us differently: Whites, Blacks, Yellow, Rulers, and the ruled. Intellectually, we are superior to the Blacks; that has been proven beyond any reasonable doubt over the years. I believe that the Afrikaner is an honest, God-fearing person who has demonstrated practically the right way of being.

Nevertheless, it is comforting to know that behind the scenes, Europe, America, Canada, Australia – and all others are behind us in spite of what they say. For diplomatic relations, we all know what language should be used and where.

To prove my point, Comrades, does anyone of you know a White country without an investment or interest in South Africa? Who buys our gold? Who buys our diamonds? Who trades with us? Who is helping us to develop other nuclear weapons? The very truth is that we are their people, and they are our people. It's a big secret. The strength of our economy is backed by America, Britain, and Germany.

It is our strong conviction, therefore, that Black is the RAW material for THE WHITE MAN. So Brothers and Sisters, let us join hands together to fight against this Black devil. I appeal to all Afrikaners to come out with any creative means of fighting this war. Surely God cannot forsake his own people whom we are. By now, every one of us has seen practically that the Blacks cannot rule themselves.

Give them guns, and they will kill each other. They are good at nothing else but making noise, dancing, marrying many wives, and indulging in sex. Let us all accept that the Black man is the symbol of poverty, mental inferiority, laziness, and emotional incompetence. Isn't it plausible, therefore, that the White man is created to rule the Black man? Come to think of what would happen one day if you woke up and on the throne sat a Kaffir! (Negar). Can you imagine what would happen to our women? Does anyone of you believe that the Blacks can rule this country?..........

Lightning Source UK Ltd.
Milton Keynes UK
UKHW020031110123
415109UK00015B/1022